The PRAYER
That Works

The
PRAYER
That Works

Ayodeji David Olusanmi

Copyright

The Prayer That Works
by Ayodeji David Olusnmi

Cover design by LisaHainline.com
Interior design and editing by CraftingStones.com

Copyright © 2011 by Ayodeji David Olusanmi

ISBN: 978-1-61364-910-7

Contact Copyright Holder at

Ayodeji D. Olusanmi
Baruch Publishing
152 Oval Road North
Dagenham, Essex
RM10 9EH
England
a.ilesanmi85@yahoo.co.uk

All Rights Reserved. No part of this publication may be reproduced, stored in a retrieval system, or transmitted in any form or by any means without the express written consent of copyright holder.

Unless otherwise noted, all Scripture quotations are taken from the King James Version of the Holy Bible, which is in the public domain.

Scripture noted AMP are taken from the Amplified Bible, Copyright © 1954, 1958, 1962, 1964, 1965, 1987 by The Lockman Foundation. All rights reserved.

Scriptures noted NLT are taken from the Holy Bible. New Living Translation copyright© 1996, 2004, 2007 by Tyndale House Foundation. All rights reserved.

Dedication

In the fulfilment of a promise made, I dedicate this book to Oluwatoyin Ilesanmi, a lovely sister. It's my prayer that you will walk in the footsteps of Susanna Wesley, bringing forth children of destiny who will possess the gates of their enemies; hence, becoming a mother of nations.

You're a jewel!

And they blessed Rebekah, and said unto her, Thou art our sister, be thou the mother of thousands of millions, and let thy seed possess the gate
of those which hate them.

~ Genesis 24:60

Contents

Foreword ix
The Two Pillars of Christianity 1
1. **The Prayer** *That Is Effectual and Fervent* 7
2. **The Prayer** *from the Heart* 17
3. **The Prayer** *of Abode* 29
4. **The Prayer** *from the Righteous* 37
5. **The Prayer** *with Sincere Motive* 53
6. **The Prayer** *in the Spirit* 57
7. **The Prayer** *of a Soul Winner* 75
8. **The Prayer** *That Is Continuous* 89
9. **The Prayer** *That Is Unified* 101
Notes 113
Acknowledgments 115
About the Author 117

Foreword

"Ask, and it shall be given you; seek, and ye shall find; knock, and it shall be opened unto you" (Matt. 7:7). The Holy Word of God is not a suggestion. It is a commandment. And greater still (John 1:50) in the realm of prayer is the level where you *go beyond* knocking and like federal agents on a drug bust, you kick in the door and storm into the throne room of grace.

"Who is this that has rudely interrupted me and has provoked my attention by his disturbance?" asks the Lord. It's Abraham! It's Jacob! It's Rachel! It's Moses! It's Joshua! It's Samson! It's Hannah! It's David! It's Elijah! It's Elisha! It's Isaiah! It's Esther! It's Daniel! It's Nehemiah! It's Anna! It's Jesus! It's the Persistent Widow! It's James! It's Paul! It's Cornelius! It's Epaphras! It's David Brainerd! It's Robert Mcheyne! It's Martin Luther! It's Praying Payson! It's John Fletcher! It's E. M. Bounds! It's Father Nash! It's J. A. Babalola! It's Ayodeji Olusanmi. It's the praying men and women of God! And I pray that it is you!

The Prayer that Works is the prayer that's quickened by the passion of Christ; the prayer that works is the prayer that's in constant communion with God; the prayer that works is the prayer that seeks the heart of God; the prayer that works is the desperate prayer that demands and commands a response from Him who answers by fire; the prayer that works is a prayer that provokes divine attention and intervention; the prayer

Foreword

that works is the prayer that transcends lip service (Matt. 6:7; Mark 7:6) and lifeless religious motions and vibrancies; the prayer that works are deep sighs and groanings in the spirit; the prayer that works is the conversation of the righteous heart with God; the prayer that works is the prayer that seeks beyond the hands of God; the prayer that works is the prayer that seeks the mind of God; the prayer that works is the prayer that seeks the will of God; the prayer that works is the prayer in secret; the prayer that works is the prayer that has no respect for geographic locations, social/religious conditions or the hypocritical ways of men; the prayer that works is the prayer that cuts through barriers and knows no bounds; the prayer that works boils from deep knowledge of the holy; the prayer that works is the point where the pursued becomes the pursuer (be it you or God!); the prayer that works agonizes, it's the prayer that's troubling; the prayer that works is a strange cry to the hearers; the prayer that works is the prayer that gets hell's attention; the prayer that works is a spectacle both to demons and angels; the prayer that works flows from the honest heart; the prayer that works comes from the broken and contrite spirit; the prayer that works is the prayer of the penitent sinner; the prayer that works is the prayer that seeks God's glory; the prayer that works is the prayer that's consistent and persistent; the prayer that works comes from the heart that is full of love and compassion; the prayer that works is self-LESS; the prayer that works is offered up in tears; the prayer that works is the sacrifice of the righteous; the prayer that works is the genuine prayer inspired and muscled by the Holy Spirit of God.

Foreword

This book comes in the desperate need of the hour. Never in the history of the Church of Jesus Christ has she appeared to be so powerless. We go about begging, building machineries, and depending on the arm of flesh (man). Why? Because we have lost Holy Ghost power. But ask yourself. How much of that did the early Church have? They had nothing and didn't beg! Actually, they had *one* thing, and that was the Holy Ghost—without whom there is no true prayer. These lay men and women turned the whole world upside down! It was the people who went out of their way to sell their possessions and bring the monies—not to give to the apostles but to lay it down at their feet.

The world was at their feet and at their mercy. Holy passion was in motion—but don't get carried away because it all started in the Upper Room—at the place of concentrated prayers (Acts 1:14). For ten days they were shut in, in prayers and fastings. Dear Pastor, when last was *your* local assembly troubled by her spiritual mess and in holy anger you called a ten-day prayer meeting to repent and seek God's face? How many would show up for such meeting? The problem of the Church is still in the pulpit and not in the pew! The ministers are the culprits (Joel 2:17). The leaders cause the people to err (Isa. 9:16). Tarrying meetings are almost extinct.

The Church of Jesus Christ was born into the world to manifest the kingdom of God and to rescue perishing souls, but now the kingdom of man and Satan are being manifested in the Church; so much so that there is not much difference between the Church and the world. The birds of the same feathers still flock together.

Foreword

O Saints of God, where are the remnant–the troubled ones, the holy minority, the consecrated ones who have renounced and denounced the lust of the world and the ways of men, the ones who abhor what now passes to be the Church of Jesus Christ and in holy anger shut themselves away in secret prayer for God to bow the heavens and come down? It begins at the place of hot spurring prayers and the starting point is where the heart is troubled and dissatisfied by the present situation.

The Prayer that Works is a prayer that is pleasing to God. The message of Brother Ayodeji is for the prayer altar to be built again—and this time *correctly*. And the only hope you have to hear it and get the spirit behind the message is if the Holy Spirit of God comes and kindles it in your heart. Your prayers can either be a stench in God's nostrils or a sweet smelling perfume. It can either cause sorrow to the kingdom of darkness or earn its ridicule.

   Elijah A. Lamb
   Author of *The Portrait of a Prophet*

The Two Pillars of Christianity

The ministry of a Christian as a whole is upheld by two vital forces—prayer and the word of God. One is not greater than the other. In fact, they are complementary. In the absence of one, the other does not function properly. Just as human beings walk on their two legs, to walk only on one is to make slow progress, and then comes a full stop.

The first pillar is that of prayer. The power–ability-that prayer generates for a believer is beyond human comprehension. Quite a number of things that God did for man was by the means of prayer; and quite a number of things that God would still do for man is still by the means of prayer.

God is a God of agenda; however, praying men and women determine if His agenda will be executed here on earth, or not. If men would pray, then men would see God. God reaches men through praying men. To be prayerless is to have none of God's attributes in operation. Love, peace, joy, humility, brokenness, faith, hope, and longsuffering are all fruits of the operation of the Holy Spirit in the life of a believer through prayer.

To be without prayer is to be without fruits. A prayerless believer is a fruitless and giftless believer. The gift of God is stirred up through prayer. A believer is expected to be filled with the knowledge of God's will in all wisdom and spiritual understanding. He is expected to live a life worthy of the Lord that he may please Him. He is expected to be strengthened with all might according to His glorious power, unto all patience and longsuffering with joyfulness. All these expectations will weary a prayerless believer because he is expected to attain it through prayer. Prayer is that which enables man to access the glory realm of the Almighty.

Smith Wigglesworth, a pioneer of the Pentecostal Revival in the early 1900s, told the story of a woman who said her husband was very stubborn and would not come to Christ. There came a day when the couple had an argument and the husband left the house. The wife called on Wigglesworth who assured her that her husband will return that night (usually when they had a fight the husband would not come home until some days later).

Wigglesworth told her that when he comes home, she should serve the husband his choice meal and allow him go to bed. Afterwards, she should go and pray in the Spirit and enter into glory, after which she should go lay hands on him and claim his soul for Christ. The husband came home that same night. The woman obeyed what Wigglesworth said and that led to his salvation. That is how potent prayer is.

The lifeline of potent prayer is the word of God—the second pillar of Christianity. To pray without the word is an abomination. Any prayer that has no root in the word of God will not be answered by God. He pays no attention to such. There is no legal ground upon which His attention can be secured.

The word of God in the Scriptures is likened to wood; and to make a successful bonfire, you need wood. You need to continuously put in the wood because where there is no wood there would soon be no fire (Prov.

26:20). Imperatively, the fire is needed for spiritual vibrancy.

Why do you think the apostles in Acts chapter 6 refused to spend their time serving tables? They knew that the source of their power and effectiveness in ministry was spending time in prayer and the word of God. They knew that man shall not live by bread alone but by every word that proceeds out of the mouth of God. That tells me that he who has no word in his spirit is dead while he lives.

According to divine purpose, a man is supposed to draw his living essentially from the word of God because the word is Spirit and life. Any other source leads to decay and death. The apostles did not want to die, hence they cried out saying, "We will give ourselves continually to prayer, and to the ministry of the word" (Acts 6:4).

Let's focus our thoughts on the word "continually." The apostles said they would give themselves continually to prayer. Notice that they said, *"We will give ourselves,"* which suggests that prayer is an act of will. They purposed it within themselves, in their heart. They knew the immense benefit that is attached to it.

The word "continually" also means that prayer was not something the apostles did haphazardly—neither was it done casually. It was not a Sunday to Sunday obligation—neither was it a Wednesday night religious activity. No. It was what they lived from morning to evening, Sunday to Sunday.

Why does there exist such a vast difference between the level of power the apostles operated in and what we operate in now? The answer is found throughout the book of Acts. Whenever I read it, I am greatly challenged and left wondering if we actually serve the same God. The answer is yes. We serve the same God and He does not change, but man does.

History has proven that the sacrifices our early fathers in the faith paid (which granted them the privilege to walk in such a glorious powerful realm) are not being paid by modern day Christians—us.

Many believers are minding tables, being concerned about religious activities, while the real food passes way. We have been called to be fruitful and not merely busy; hence, any seemingly good work that does not bear fruit is actually a dead work in disguise, and it deserves to be repented of. So before you blame God for unanswered prayers, check inwardly. If you are a leader, spiritually dry, do you expect God to work wonders amidst your followers? Like priest; like people. The leader gets soaked; all get wet.

The word of God is paramount to successful praying. He who knows the word knows the mind of God unhindered. The treasures of heaven are at his disposal. He has the golden key into the hidden riches of God. The consciousness of God's word allows the believer to know *when, how, where, why,* and *what* to pray. He is guided; he would not cross the line into heresy. There is a lot of funny, dangerous, and heretical praying in the body of Christ, and I believe that it is traceable to lack of the knowledge of the Scriptures. Error is unavoidable with a believer that lacks proper knowledge of God's word.

It is my prayer that as you read on, your eyes of understanding will be opened to grasp the truths presented in this book and that you will give adequate priority to God's word and prayer.

The effectual fervent prayer . . . availeth much.

~ James 5:16

1

The
PRAYER
That is Effectual and Fervent

He who prays without fervency does not pray at all. We cannot commune with God who is a consuming fire (Deuteronomy 4:24), if there is no fire in our prayers.

~ Charles H. Spurgeon

Spurgeon is right on point and, above all, he personally knew what it is to pray fervently. His achievements as a profound theologian and writer bear witness that he was a man of prayer. Whenever I read about men who had been mightily used by God, I find that they were men of prayer. All of them. They prayed fervently. Hence they got things done quickly and seemingly cheaply.

HEROES OF FAITH

It was said of Ayodele Babalola, founder of Christ Apostolic Church in Nigeria in the early 1950s, that when he prayed it would sound like a rushing mighty wind. One day, while he prayed on a mountain, a big snake fastened itself to him, but God told him to close his eyes and continue praying. It was said that by the end of the prayer session, the big snake had dried up! [1]

David Brainerd, an American missionary to Native American Indians in the early 1700s, had a similar experience. He had been wrestling with God in prayers when a rattlesnake lifted up its head to strike him; but after a few minutes of fervent prayer, it swiftly moved away. This led to a massive success in his ministry toward the Cherokee Indians because they saw the incident happen while they were on his trail to kill him. He was eventually given a prophetic welcome and the word of God spread freely throughout the tribe—all because of fervent prayer.[2]

The word "fervent" in Greek is zeó and actually means "boil." From Science class, you may remember that there is a boiling point and a melting point. Certain substances boil and certain objects melt when it reaches a particular temperature. That is how it is in the spiritual realm, too. When you pray, at a certain point, you begin to boil and melt away the enemy—the devil will take to his heels at this point because he knows that to stay around you is to be destroyed! I have been privileged to be there and I know how it feels.

"Fervent" is also translated from the Greek word, agōnizomenos meaning "agonize." Paul affirmed the intercessory ministry of Epaphras by saying, "Epaphras, who is one of you, a servant of Christ, saluteth you, always labouring fervently [fight] for you in prayers, that ye may stand perfect and complete in all the will of God" (Col. 4:12).

Dwight L. Moody, founder of Moody Bible Institute and Moody Publishers, had a financial need in the ministry. He proceeded to tell his fellow ministers how he would meet that need—through fervent prayer. When the time came for John G. Lake to move to Africa, he and a beloved brother prayed fervently. God responded to Moody and Lake by providing the finances at the time it was needed. To these men and many more, prayer was their lifeline; it should be for us too, for he that is not great in prayer is not great at all.

It was said of Martin Luther that he knew what it was to travail in prayer, to offer an effective, fervent prayer that was dynamic in its working. He knew how to wrestle with the powers of darkness. He prayed fervently every day. And once, while this great man of God prayed, he was spied on to be killed, but the spy reported back to his employer that Luther had prayed nearly all night; hence, he said that he was unable to conquer him. He became untouchable to the powers of darkness due to his fervency on the altar of prayer.[3]

How about you? Can the powers of darkness harass you? How fervent is your prayer? Ardent enough to chase away devils?

A MAN OF LIKE PASSION

James 5:16-18

Confess your faults one to another, and pray one for another, that ye may be healed. The effectual fervent prayer of a righteous man availeth much. Elias was a man subject to like passions as we are, and **he prayed earnestly** *that it might not rain: and it rained not on the earth by the space of three years and six months. And he prayed again, and the heaven gave rain, and the earth brought forth her fruit.*

Elias (also known as Elijah) was a man of prayer and we know the manner by which he prayed. In 1 Kings Chapter 17, Elijah prophesied the drought that lasted three and half years. In chapter 18, when it was time for the abundance of rain—we see how he prayed: "Elijah went up to the top of Carmel; and he cast himself down upon the earth, and put his face between his knees" (v. 42).

The NLT translation says it like this: "Elijah climbed to the top of Mount Carmel [separation] and bowed low to the ground [concentration] and prayed with his face between his knees [determination]."

POSTURE IN PRAYER

It's not my intention to tell you what posture to take in prayer. Posture in itself does not get prayer answered. God looks at the heart. When you call from your heart to Him, then He will honour you. However, our posture in prayer says a lot about our attitude, seriousness, and determination.

On the other hand is the religious belief that God hears quicker, perhaps better when one lies down or kneels. However, God honours and hears faith which proceeds out of a pure heart. He heard Christ whenever He prayed. Yet, the Scriptures never report whether Christ was lying down or kneeling when he prayed at the tomb of Lazarus or during His great priestly prayer of John chapter 17.

We do know, though, that Christ was a man of fervent prayer. It takes fervency to sweat while praying—He prayed and His sweat was like drops of blood falling to the ground (Luke 22:44). Ordinary prayers would not have caused His transfiguration. It was a result of fervent prayer. *"As he prayed, the fashion of his countenance was altered, and his raiment was white and glistering"* (Luke 9:29). A weakling at the altar of prayer cannot avail much because the effectual and fervent prayer of a man avails much!

Having said all this, I believe Christ was a Man who took a Spirit-driven posture whenever He prayed. We should also endeavour to take a posture as led by the Spirit of God. This means, don't kneel down to pray when you know you could be taken over by sleep. It would be better to pace or go for a prayer walk—whatever it takes to pray with and in the Spirit. Personally, when I'm impressed upon by the Spirit to take a certain posture in prayer, I do it; otherwise, I prefer go for a prayer walk.

Elijah's Posture

Everything we find in the Scripture is meaningful no matter how small or irrelevant it may appear. The Bible giving us the picture of Elijah's posture while he prayed means a lot. We do not know if this is his pattern of praying or just a one-time occurrence. Sensitivity to the Spirit is essential. Our posture should depict true worship; it should show how reverential we are toward God. We cannot behold His almightiness and take a funny posture. The angels are bowing down to worship. The twenty-four elders cast down their crowns before the King of kings. The presence of God must be treated with utmost respect. This generation knows little about that. We must decrease for Him to increase. We must stay down for Him to go up.

Culture, Posture, and Scripture

In some cultures, a child must approach an elder with a deep sense of honour and respect. In the Yoruba culture of Nigeria, for example, the male child prostrates to greet an elder, while the female child kneels down. These postures reflect submission and adoration. This practice is also scriptural. When a child refuses to show this kind of respect, he or she is deemed rebellious, arrogant, and proud and said to "lack home training." Such a child brings shame to the whole family.

When we approach God in a reverential manner of posture with an adequate knowledge of what we are doing, it makes tremendous power available to us. Numerous men of God were said to live on their knees, David Livingstone, Scottish missionary to Africa in the early 1800s is an example. It's widely reported that he was found dead on his knees in prayer.

Is it not true that some of us come into the presence of God with levity? Some chew gum, others lay half asleep. God is not mocked. Whatsoever a man sows, the same shall he reap. When you sow seriousness, God becomes committed to your prayers. When you sow otherwise, He becomes otherwise with you. Do you not know that much *fervent* prayer equals *dynamic* power? Much *fervent* prayer equals much grace, which equals greater works.

If the man of God—Elijah—had not taken a serious, determined approach on that mountain, what do you suppose would have happened? Nothing. No rain. No abundance. It would be as though God never spoke.

Many people have heard from God like Elijah did, but how reverentially and fervently are they praying? What approach are they taking toward God's promises for their life? To be sluggish and weak at the altar of prayer is to be a loser in life.

Now Hannah, she spake in her heart; only her lips moved, but her voice was not heard: therefore Eli thought she had been drunken.

~ 1 Sam. 1:13

2

The PRAYER
from the Heart

Trust in him at all times; ye people, pour out your heart before him: God is a refuge for us.

~ Psalm 62:8

There is something unique and supernatural about the spirit of a man. It has an unquantifiable capacity to achieve whatever it determines to do. Permit me to say that the spirit of the man is also the heart of the man—which is the man himself. Jesus said that out of the heart—the real you—proceeds the issues of life, both good and bad (Matthew 15:11-20). We are constantly warned in the Holy Scriptures to guide our heart with all diligence because everything we become in life emanates from it—the heart.

I will endeavour to explain the spirit of the man or "the heart of a man" better still the man himself—how it functions using this natural illustration: I remember the story of a young boy who at a tender age had the privilege of entering into the office of executive personnel. As one would expect, it was elegant and quite desirable.

The young boy liked what he saw and something in him, which was the "real him" said, "One day I'm going to have an office just like this." These words came out of his very being, from his heart, the real man himself. It was a desperate yearning of the heart. A pouring out of the soul. No man heard him and the same was true for Hannah: *"Now Hannah, she spake in her heart; only her lips moved, but her voice was not heard."* But God heard the pouring out of Hannah's heart and He heard the pouring out of this boy's heart and He stamped it with approval. By age thirty, John Graham Lake was presented an office exactly the same as he had seen as a young boy.

The story of Hannah is also the story of a mother pouring out her heart in prayer. Hannah was the mother of one of Israel's most prominent prophets—Samuel. She was also greatly beloved of her husband but ridiculed for being barren. Two factors moved Hannah into action to remedy that: first, she was getting old and, second, she had already been married a considerable length of time without producing a child.

To put our discussion in a proper context and have a better understanding, let's read her story directly from the Scripture so we can understand her prayer from the heart, which is *the prayer that works*.

The Prayer *from the Heart*

1 Samuel 1:7-18

As he did so year by year, when she went up to the house of the LORD, so she provoked her; therefore she wept, and did not eat. Then said Elkanah her husband to her, Hannah, why weepest thou? and why eatest thou not? and why is thy heart grieved? am not I better to thee than ten sons?

So Hannah rose up after they had eaten in Shiloh, and after they had drunk. Now Eli the priest sat upon a seat by a post of the temple of the LORD. And she was in bitterness of soul, and prayed unto the LORD, and wept sore. And she vowed a vow, and said, O LORD of hosts, if thou wilt indeed look on the affliction of thine handmaid, and remember me, and not forget thine handmaid, but wilt give unto thine handmaid a man child, then I will give him unto the LORD all the days of his life, and there shall no razor come upon his head. And it came to pass, as she continued praying before the LORD, that Eli marked her mouth.

Now Hannah, she spake in her heart; only her lips moved, but her voice was not heard: therefore Eli thought she had been drunken. And Eli said unto her, How long wilt thou be drunken? put away thy wine from thee. And Hannah answered and said, No, my lord, I am a woman of a sorrowful spirit: I have drunk neither wine nor strong drink, but have poured out my soul before the LORD. Count not thine handmaid for a daughter of Belial: for out of the abundance of my complaint and grief have I spoken hitherto.

Then Eli answered and said, Go in peace: and the God of Israel grant thee thy petition that thou hast asked of him. And she said, Let thine handmaid find grace in thy sight. So the woman went her way, and did eat, and her countenance was no more sad.

THE POURING OUT OF THE SOUL

Samuel the great Prophet of Israel was poured out of the soul of his mother, Hannah. Samuel became a reality because Hannah genuinely poured out her soul unto God. She said to Eli, *"No, my lord, I am a woman of a sorrowful spirit: I have drunk neither wine nor strong drink,* **but have poured out my soul before the LORD.** *Count not thine handmaid for a daughter of Belial: for out of the abundance of my complaint and grief have I spoken hitherto."*

In the beginning God made Adam to sleep and God took a rib out of Adam and made Eve. God poured out Eve through the being of Adam. So it's not a surprise to read Adam's comment when he saw Eve: *"This is now bone of my bones, and flesh of my flesh; she shall be called 'woman,'* **for she was taken out of man**" (See Gen. 2:21-23). Though Adam *did not* pray for a wife, however, within man is the power—the ability—for productivity if he will properly harness his potential; and the same was true for Hannah.

Hannah *did* pray for a male child, and God brought forth prophet Samuel from her very self. Hence, her response to the birth is not surprising. She named her son Samuel, meaning "asked of God," saying, *"I have asked him of the LORD"* (1 Sam. 1:20).

THE GOD OF ISRAEL GRANTS YOUR HEART'S DESIRE

Hannah poured out herself unto God and, having been mistaken for a drunkard, a comforting word broke forth from the throne of grace. Eli the Priest, who is a symbol of God's authority, said these edifying words to Hannah, *"The God of Israel grant thee thy petition that thou hast asked of him."* So Hannah went on her way, eating and no longer looking sad.

Precious saints, these right words that came to Hannah in due season did not come from the throne of grace out of nowhere. If we are to be beneficiaries of such promises from God, we must learn to pour out our souls to Him like Hannah did. We must pray from our hearts because God reckons with the heart. When a man speaks directly and sincerely from his heart and his desires are in line with the will of God, he commands heaven's attention and gets whatever he wants (see 1 John 5:14-15). The book of Matthew tells of a woman who received such a comforting promise from our Lord Jesus:

Matthew 9:20-22

Behold, a woman, which was diseased with an issue of blood twelve years, came behind him, and touched the hem of his garment: **For she said within herself,** *If I may but touch his garment, I shall be whole. But Jesus turned him about, and when he saw her, he said, Daughter, be of good comfort; thy faith hath made thee whole. And the woman was made whole from that hour.*

The Prayer *That Works*

Reading from verse 21, we clearly see how this woman received her healing: she poured out herself to God within her heart. The Scriptures give us her petition: **"*For she said within herself,* *If I may but touch his garment, I shall be whole."*** And in verse 22, the seal of heaven came upon the heartfelt request: *"Jesus turned him about, and when he saw her, he said, Daughter, be of good comfort; thy faith hath made thee whole. And the woman was made whole from that hour."*

Beloved, such sweet words as these are found without reserve in the bosom of the Father, who is seeking whom He may say it to. Until we first pour out our hearts, such words won't come.

Oh, how I long to see the day when believers will pray indeed *like* believers. If every genuine, believing soul would pour their soul out to God, such words as "be of good comfort," "rejoice I have overcome the world," "weep not," and "God grants your heart desire," would flow down from heaven. Heaven has no need of it, but you and I do in this present evil world.

Let me add that these are not words that are spoken from heaven on a plate of gold. Hannah got her answer only after she had fasted, wept, and determined within herself to be healed. The woman with the issue of blood got her own desire fulfilled after she came to the end of herself and had pressed through the crowd to touch the Saviour. Believers that are full of themselves will never touch God because He resists the proud.

In the days of the prophets, the priests would tear their clothes to show sorrow and even anger over their sins. If, today, we would tear apart our hearts and not our clothes, God's words would rain down on us, too. Every time I have approached the throne of grace in repentance, fasting, worshiping, and praying—heaven opens and answer to requests come quicker than expected. This is our heritage as children of the most high. We however, need to rise up to the challenge and lay hold of what is ours, by force. Heaven hears the forceful. The heartfelt prayer avails much!

Travailing – A Sure Means of Salvation

Isaiah 66:8

Who hath heard such a thing? who hath seen such things? Shall the earth be made to bring forth in one day? or shall a nation be born at once? ***for as soon as Zion travailed, she brought forth her children.***

I remember a story about how one of William Booth's men (of the Salvation Army) came back dejected, defeated, and discouraged from the missionary field. Souls were not being saved at the expected rate, so he came back to meet Booth that he might quit the work of the ministry. After a long conversation, Booth said to him, "Try tears." In other words, pour out your heart to God.

This man of God knew what tears can do whenever they're poured out of a genuine soul. He knew, for instance, that if Zion would truly travail, she would prevail. If she would travail, she would bring forth her children. We are not prevailing because we are not travailing. A travailing soul is a prevailing soul!

Another story was told by the Bible school teacher, Dr Edward Miller, in his book, *Cry for Me Argentina*, in which he narrated how he believes the Argentine revival of the 1950s came to be. He said that a young group of students with a burden for intercession had been meeting days after days, praying. He said those prayer meetings were marked by tears, repentance, prophetic words, and angelic visitations with a definite message from the Lord.

He told of how each student poured out his soul to God in prayer for the salvation of Argentina. Before this point, Argentina had no idea of what I call *true religion*. Argentines were caught up in idolatry, immorality, paganism, Catholicism. Nothing real. They had no idea that Jesus is the only saviour. Then, when the days of weeping were divinely coming to an end, a word came from the Lord telling them not to weep again and that the Lion of the tribe of Judah has prevailed over the prince of Argentina. That was what they needed to hear. It was a point of breakthrough.

Two years later, according to the word of the Lord, real revival broke out in Argentina. Evangelistic crusades were filled to the brim. Stadiums that sat up to 180,000 persons could not contain the amount of people that were now yearning for the word of life. What started so seemingly insignificant with these young groups of students, marked a great change in the history of Argentina.[1]

ARE YOU PREGNANT?

As soon as Zion travailed, she brought forth her children. The word "travailed" in Isaiah 66:8 has something to do with a woman being pregnant. It describe a woman in labour, trying to bring forth a child into the world. Jerusalem, the mother of us all is said to have entered into labour. She is travailing. Her water broke and she brought forth—that is, delivered—souls into the kingdom.

This means that if we are going to bring forth souls, everyone in Zion (God's kingdom) ought to be pregnant—that is, have visions for souls that would send us into our closet for intercession, which would eventually birth revival and usher in a mass exodus of souls into Zion. If there is going to be travailing and multiplication of souls in Zion, then there must first be pregnancies. When we enter our closet, intercede, and travail for the lost souls, the moment of delivery will come.

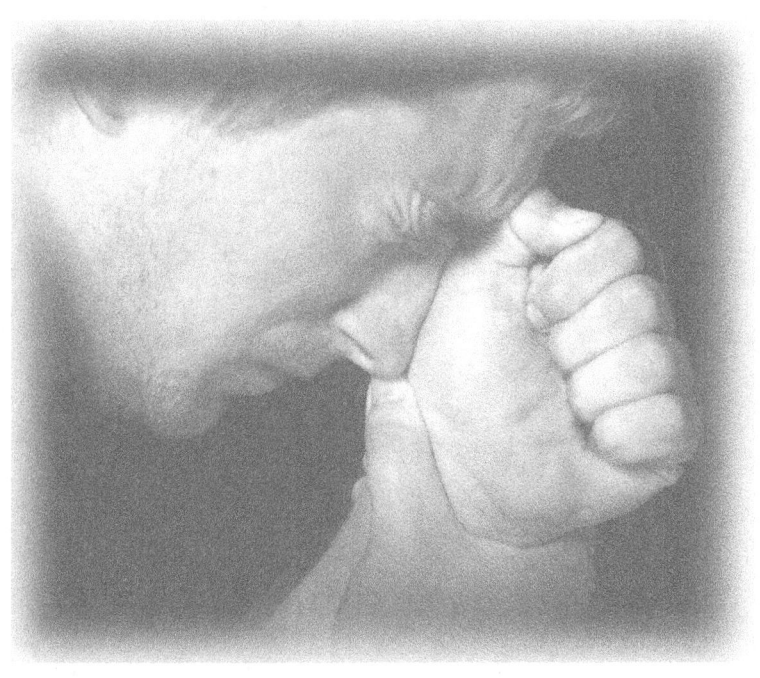

*If ye abide in me, and my words abide in you,
ye shall ask what ye will,
and it shall be done unto you*

~ John 15:7

3

The
PRAYER
of Abode

If ye abide in me, and my words abide in you, ye shall ask what ye will, and it shall be done unto you

~ John 15:7

The prayer of abode is a prayer that works because the word of God dwells richly within us. Such word-based prayer works because the Word of Life is in our very being. God gave precise instructions to His servant Joshua regarding His word; these instructions are still applicable to us today if we care to be mighty in God's hand (see Joshua 1:1-9) and if we want to defeat the enemy of our soul.

I once heard about the confession of a lady involved in witchcraft. She told of every atrocity perpetrated in her demonic group. She said that the only people the kingdom of darkness respects are those believers who use the word of God whenever they are praying—those that have the right word for the right petition. Her confession was not strange to me; all you need to do is open your Bible to Matthew chapter 4. There Jesus Christ defeats Satan with nothing but the words of God. Jesus Christ said to Satan, "It is written."

"Of course," you might say. "He knew the word because He was the word." That is not totally right. Though He was the word, He still had to read the words. The Gospel of Luke chapter 4 verse 16 mentions a custom of Christ: *"He came to Nazareth, where he had been brought up: and,* **as his custom was***, he went into the synagogue on the sabbath day, and stood up for to read."* He had a usual pattern of going to the synagogue to read the Scriptures; He was someone we could refer to as a lay reader.

How far are we from this sort of custom? Though we have various translations of the Bible, how many of us genuinely sit down to study them? Where are the Bereans? Instead, we are satisfied with little or no knowledge of the Saviour. We are satisfied with a few words from daily devotional books, and we expect our prayer to work? Devotional books are useful, but they don't substitute for the word of God.

You see, the devil is not scared about how many study Bibles we have no matter how rich their commentaries may be. He is only scared when we store the Scriptures in our heart. Have you read the psalmist who said, "Thy word I have hidden in my heart that I may not sin against thee"? Putting the God's words in our heart puts the devil at bay.

IF YE ABIDE IN ME AND MY WORDS ABIDE IN YOU

Jesus gave His disciples another key to prevailing prayer when He told them, "Abide in me and my words abide in you." He was saying to them, "Let my word dwell in you richly." When His word is in you, you would know what to ask, you would not ask amiss. You would be able to discern the will of God. You would know what is good, acceptable, and perfect. To abide in His word is to abide in Him because in the beginning was the word and the word was with God and the word was God.

APPEARING OR ABIDING

Samuel the prophet not only appeared before the Lord, he abode there. Many of us appear in Church on Sunday morning. We sing praises to the Lord and read our Bible when the preacher comes on, but we are not abiding in His presence during the week. We read our Bibles once a week and we wonder why we are spiritually weak. We feed on junk food during the week and expect a quick fix and makeover on Sunday morning. It does not happen like that, beloved.

We have turned our pastors into magicians expecting them to do for us what we do not do for ourselves. Your pastor cannot help you any further than you are willing to help yourself. Do not expect to be mighty in prayer when during the week you feed on garbage. You might know more about video games, television shows, and sporting events than you do about God and His word, and you expect to triumph in life? No brother! No sister! It doesn't work that way. Let us see how it worked for Samuel.

The Prayer *That Works*

1 Samuel 1:22

*But Hannah went not up; for she said unto her husband, I will not go up until the child be weaned, and then I will bring him, **that he may appear before the LORD, and there [before the LORD] abide for ever.***

1 Samuel 3:19-21

*And Samuel grew, and the LORD was with him, **and did let none of his words fall to the ground**. And all Israel from Dan even to Beersheba knew that Samuel was established to be a prophet of the LORD. And the LORD appeared again in Shiloh: for the LORD revealed himself to Samuel in Shiloh by the word of the LORD.*

Hannah, in order to fulfil the vow she made to God concerning her son, brought the child Samuel before the Lord that he may appear there and abide forever. Hannah did this because she knew the importance of the presence of the Lord. She was a mother that valued the atmosphere of His being. That is why I agree with Charles Spurgeon who said that he could not be convinced that a mother who does not bring her children to church would bring them to Christ. Perhaps it takes more effort to come to Christ than go to church.

Let us see the reward of God's presence in Samuel's ministry. First, the Lord was with him. The Scripture that says, "Draw near to Me and I will draw near to you"[1] was fulfilled in his life.

Second, Samuel's words—prayers, petitions, and prophecies—never fell to the ground. God honoured them because he who honours God, the same God will honour him.

The third benefit Samuel enjoyed was that he had a *firsthand* revelation of God Himself. By firsthand revelation of God, I mean that Samuel did not go around proclaiming and living in someone else's rhema (God-spoken word). He had his own rhema. He did not just know *about* God, he received a fresh revelation from God. *"For the LORD revealed himself to Samuel in Shiloh by the word of the LORD."* Many of us know *about God,* we do not *know God.* We must have a revelation of the word of God to truly know God.

Unfortunately, many of us go about our day quoting what God said to brother so and so, but we do not have a *now* word for ourselves. We cannot grow like that. For our prayer to work, we must receive a revelation from the word while abiding in it. This revelation and illumination will not come to us if we do not abide. God's sacred revelations are not cheap; they are not easy to come by. Prophet Habakkuk had to stand on his watch to hear and see what the Lord would say to him (Hab. 2:1.), and so have many effective men and women of prayer.

The story of revivalists reveal that they treasured the presence of God and His word above every other thing. They were like the apostle Paul who declared *"I count all things but loss for the excellency of the knowledge of Christ Jesus my Lord"* (Phil. 3:8).

The apostle of faith, as people call Smith Wigglesworth, said he would give anyone that found him without his New Testament Bible a certain amount of money. Do you wonder why his prayer of faith worked so well and why we are still talking about it?

The revelation from Acts 10:38 produced both John Alexander Dowie and John Graham Lake, for God was with these great men. Likewise, it was said that Charles G. Finney walked into a cotton factory one day and God, through Finney's appearance, convicted a woman of her sins. She immediately began crying and soon nearly all in the room burst into tears. The superintendent closed the factory for the day and Finney conducted a revival. In his autobiography, Finney recalls, "A more powerful meeting I scarcely ever attended. . . . In the course of a few days, nearly all the mill were converted."[2]

What value do you place on God's presence? Do you just appear and disappear? You appear in Church and your pastor knows you, but does God know you? You might at this point pour out your heart to God, repenting of every slothful service you have been rendering. Tell Him to take away the dross in you. Your silver must shine; anything hindering your effectiveness on the altar of prayer must be destroyed.

Let us pray, *God set me apart for a fresh walk with you. Manifest Yourself to me; be real to me. Work in and on me to Your glory alone. Make my heart, oh God, Your dwelling place. Lord, prepare me to be a sanctuary, pure, and holy, tried and true.*

*The effectual fervent prayer
of a righteous man availeth much.*

~ James 5:16

4

The PRAYER from the Righteous

The effectual fervent prayer of a righteous man availeth much.

~ James 5:16

Anyone can pray. Absolutely anyone. But do all receive expected answers to their prayers? Certainly not. Therefore, I have tagged the number four form of prayer that works as the "Prayer from the Righteous."

You might already have an idea why some of us pray and nothing seems to happen. The Scriptures says, *"The sacrifice of the wicked is abomination: how much more, when he bringeth it with a wicked mind?"* (Prov. 21:27). Prayer is a form of sacrifice. It takes real energy for real prayers. Hence we can read

Proverbs 21:27 like this: *"The prayer of the wicked is an abomination."*

Does it amaze you that the wicked or unrighteous pray? It does me. I think to myself, "Does he not know he is wicked?" There is hope for him if only he will offer quality repentance, turn to Christ for salvation, and receive His righteousness. There are two ways for him to do this.

Two Ways to Receive Righteousness

The believer is blessed of the most high. He has been endowed with what he does not merit. He enjoys divine privileges, such as Christ being made his righteousness. Believers assume His righteousness in two forms.

The body without the spirit is dead. Likewise faith without works is dead. Faith alone cannot save any man, neither does works alone. In other words, God's grace saves us and then we need to present to God both faith and works in order to receive the full benefit of our redemption package.

Therefore, the first way that a believer takes on the righteousness of God is from that which was bestowed upon him by the grace that came through Jesus Christ, the only Son of God. The Spirit of God revealed this gracious gift of righteousness through Paul when he said, "*He* [God] *hath made him* [Jesus] *to be sin for us* [Believers]*, who knew no sin; that we might be made the **righteousness** of God in him"* (2 Cor. 5:21).

Also, chapter 59 of the book of Isaiah has something to say about Christ being our righteousness. Verse 17 reads, *"This is the heritage of the servants of the LORD, and their **righteousness is of me**, saith the LORD."*

The second way a believer assumes, takes on, righteousness is by his *good* works. Oh, not many of us would like to hear that because it places a sense of responsibility on us. And if there is something we hate as humans, it is being responsible. There is a great need in these last days for spiritual responsibility. If you lack in this area, you might want to say this prayer: "Oh Lord, place upon my soul the burden for spiritual responsibility and accountability."

Let me further add that "taking on" righteousness is more of a "maintaining" of righteousness by the operation of the Holy Spirit in us. So therefore let no man glory in works. As the Scriptures points out, we are not of them that glory in their own works; we know that it is Him that is at work in us both to will and do to His good pleasure.

The good works that is manifested in our lives is spurred and driven by the Holy Spirit of God. If we are righteous, it is because He enabled us. If we are effective in His service, it is because He helped us. If we run, and soar like eagles, it is because He gave us the strength. If He does something great with our lives, we must acknowledge that it is because the purpose of Him who has been called must stand according to election. He that must boast should boast in the Lord—in what the Lord has done through him.

After reading these two paragraphs, you might ask, "Where does this author place the grace of God in the salvation process?" Be assured that this is not another legalistic book. I know and believe that a man is solely saved by the grace of God through faith in Christ, not of works. But as you continue in this chapter and you will see that I am promoting the *being of righteousness* and not merely the *doing* as Titus 2:11-12 promotes as well.

For the grace of God that bringeth salvation hath appeared to all men, Teaching us that, denying ungodliness and worldly lusts, we should live soberly, righteously, and godly, in this present world;

Let us delve into more Scriptures to validate the claim that a believer's work that is genuinely driven by the Holy-Spirit through the grace of God is paramount to an effective prayer life.

James 2:17-26

Even so faith, if it hath not works, is dead, being alone. Yea, a man may say, Thou hast faith, and I have works: shew me thy faith without thy works, and I will shew thee my faith by my works. Thou believest that there is one God; thou doest well: the devils also believe, and tremble. But wilt thou know, O vain man, that faith without works is dead? Was not Abraham our father justified by works, when he had offered Isaac his son upon the altar?

Seest thou how faith wrought with his works, and by works was faith made perfect? And the scripture was fulfilled which saith, Abraham believed God, and it was imputed unto him for righteousness: and he was called the Friend of God.

Ye see then how that by works a man is justified, and not by faith only. Likewise also was not Rahab the harlot justified by works, when she had received the messengers, and had sent them out another way?

For as the body without the spirit is dead, so faith without works is dead also.

Passages like this from the Scriptures speak to us of the responsibility that lies on the part of every believer. Yes, God has done His part and done it all, but you and I also have something to do. God's righteousness is settled in us—that's God's part, but our part is said well by Paul in 2 Corinthians 7:1: *"Let us cleanse ourselves . . . perfecting holiness in the fear of God."* We must continuously work at this cleansing and perfecting into holiness so that we all may come to the fullness of Christ's image.

The apostle John spoke even more directly about this. He established that though Christianity is the work of the Spirit from within, he stressed that the inner work must reflect on the outside. Many in his days who claimed to be saved were not living the life as expected of them. The same is happening among so-called believers in this generation. Little wonder the apostle Paul warned Titus that the people who have believed in God should be careful to maintain good works. He further stressed that this warning is good and profitable unto all men. Beware of preachers and teachers who will deceive you into a false righteousness.

LET NO MAN DECEIVE YOU OUT OF RIGHTEOUSNESS

1 John 3:7-10, 22

*Little children, **let no man deceive you**: he that doeth righteousness is righteous, even as he is righteous He that committeth sin is of the devil; for the devil sinneth from the beginning. For this purpose the Son of God was manifested, that he might destroy the works of the devil Whosoever is born of God doth not commit sin; for his seed remaineth in him: and he cannot sin, because he is born of God. In this the children of God are manifest, and the children of the devil: **whosoever doeth not righteousness is not of God. . . . And whatsoever we ask [in prayer], we receive of him**, because we keep his commandments, and **do those things** that are pleasing in his sight*

There is nothing new under heaven, the Scripture says. Men have been custodians of evil doctrines since generations past. It was happening then in the days of the apostles, so why do we think it does not happen now in our days? I do not see it stopping but increasing. No doubt, their errors have done and are still doing great damage to God's kingdom and to new babies born into the kingdom.

The apostles fought it rigorously in their days and we are expected to fight it, too—which I endeavour to do. Some preachers teach that what you do and how you do it does not matter to God. They say that God looks on the inside, not the outside. How erroneous that is. Have they forgotten that the outside is a reflection of the inside? For instance, can a man be deceptive, dubious, malicious, envious, and cruel and expect to be mighty in prayer? No. Before a man does evil, he first thinks evil. Hence we are admonished not to let anyone deceive us into a false sense of righteousness. Instead, we are to be like the Berean Christians—searching those things we have been taught to see if they are true (Acts 17:11).

RIGHTEOUSNESS IS WHAT YOU DO

To the apostle John, righteousness is not what you chant, claim, or scream. It is what you do: *"He that doeth righteousness is righteous"* (1 John 3:7). He believed that righteousness is in the being. He believed in action not just mere words. He believed that Christians are Christ and, if so, they should walk as He walked. *"He that saith he abideth in him ought himself also so to walk, even as he walked"* (1 John 2:6). The apostle James also belonged to the same school of thought. He said, ***"Even so faith, if it hath not works, is dead, being alone"*** (James 2:17) and ***"Ye see then how that by works a man is justified,*** *and not* ***by faith only"*** (James 2:24).

How many of us believe like these great apostles did? How many of us participate in this old-time way of moving God into action? How many of us believe in this old-time religion? If the new is not generating the same kind of result as the old generated, it is wisdom to neglect the new and take back the old. What I want to see in my prayers are results. But are we not still passive, carnal, and walk like children of the world?

How many still uphold this godly standard in their hearts? How many of us preach like this any longer? We desire to be used like John G. Lake, Smith

Wigglesworth, Charles G. Finney, Oswald J. Smith, but we do not really preach what they preached. These men knew the very heartbeat of God and they gave it raw to the people. They preached the real fruit of real faith, not like we do today with our "name it and claim it" mantras that possess no genuine dedication to God and His things.

We scream and shout that we want revival. We want to see His glory. We want to enter into the holy of holies. We want to enter into His inner chamber. We want to enter into His court. The list of our wants is unending. What God wants is simple, but it appears to be difficult for us to give it to Him. The flesh wants to glory itself; the flesh wants to have its way, but God wants our flesh to die and He can't kill it without our permission.

God goes where He is reverenced and honoured. The book of Hebrews shows us the standard of God in Chapter 12 where it says, *"Follow peace with all men and* **holiness, without which no man shall see the Lord.***"* There you have it. You want to see Him? Then be righteous! You want His intervention? Be Holy. You want him to answer when you call? Live a life pleasing to Him. Then you won't need to stress—He will just show up in your temple.

Remember, *"The name of the Lord is a strong tower; the [consistently] righteous man [upright and in right standing with God] runs into it and is safe, high [above evil] and strong"* (Prov. 18:10 AMP). That is one of the benefits of doing/being righteousness. God is faithful, but are we?

"Can a man be found faithful in God's eyes?" you may be wondering. Yes he can. Moses was faithful in all his house, likewise was Abraham and Samuel (See Num. 12:7, 1 Sam. 2:35.) And it is required of us to be faithful. God expects it: "It is required in stewards, that a man be found faithful" (1 Cor. 4:2).

RIGHTEOUSNESS PLEASES GOD

Whatsoever we ask, we receive of him, because we keep his commandments, and do those things that are pleasing in his sight (1 John 3:22).

Jesus is our greatest example of righteousness, and God never let Him down. His prayers always received answers from heaven. Christ was so good that He even told us how He entered into that realm so we can follow Him into it. With this knowledge, we can henceforth check ourselves whenever we ask anything from God and answers do not come.

God declared, *"This is my beloved Son, in whom I am* **well pleased"** (Matt. 3:17). God was not just pleased with His son, He was *well* pleased, meaning that God thought very well of and took great pleasure in His thoughts of Christ. Whenever God thinks of Christ, He becomes very happy.

How does Christ enter into God's domain of *well-pleasing*? Jesus tells us, *"The father* **hath not left me alone;** [because] *I do always those things that please him"* (John 8:29). Boldly and clearly it is written out in this Scripture. God was very happy with Christ not because He was His Son—but rather, because Christ knew that for the Father to remain with Him, He had to do certain things; He had to be obedient.

Righteousness pleases God and when He is pleased then He grants us whatsoever we desire. Precious saints, do not be fooled into believing the error going on now in these last days. Do not believe anyone that makes you feel at ease in Zion. A life of ease breeds hosts of falsehoods and pretences, which definitely cannot stand the test of time. Remember the Scripture says, "Woe unto them that are at ease in Zion." Zion is for action. It is never a dull place. Possessions are possessed in Zion.

NOT ALONE

With boldness the Son of God declared, *"The father **hath not left me alone"*** (John 8:29). Christ was very sure of His relationship with His father. Are you? Are you preaching without Him? Are you walking about from day to day without Him and, to worsen it, you do not know? Are you like Jesus' parents that had travelled for awhile before knowing that He was not in their company (Luke 2:39-52)?

Samson thought he still had God with him. He was told, *"The Philistines be upon thee, Samson."* He awoke from his sleep and said, *"I will go out as at other times before, and shake myself."* But he did not know that *"the Lord was departed from him"* (Judg. 16:20). Do you see yourself in Samson's image? If so, cry out to God for revival. Be like Moses: *"If thy presence go not with me carry us not up"* (Ex. 33:15).

Beloved, the journey ahead of you is too dangerous without the Father going with you. It's deadly. How sad it is when men fall at war front. They fall primarily because they were alone while among many others. Sin and death came in through Adam to the entire human race because Eve was alone. David fell into adultery because he was alone. How many brothers have fallen into the trap of Delilah because they were alone? How many destinies have been cut short because they were alone? How many believers have been bitten by the serpent because they were alone?

All these defeats could only have happened and did happen because they were alone. The Father had left them and they knew it not.

Can you imagine how disastrous it would have been for Christ to be alone? One thing is certain: the redemptive work of Christ would not have been completed.

Without the Father, our prayers will not be answered. Until we come out of ourselves, no spiritual endeavour will work. Nothing worked for the prodigal son as long as he was outside his jurisdiction. As long as he chose to follow his own ways, he could not please his father. Any requests he made would have been thrown back at him. But when the rebellious and wayward son repented and returned to his father, the father restored him to his right standing. How blessed is the Father God we serve. We, also, can be restored back to right standing with our Father in heaven and enjoy our once lost privileges of answers to prayer—prayers of righteous men and women with sincere motives.

Ye ask, and receive not, because ye ask amiss, that ye may consume it upon your lusts.

~ James 4:3

5

The
PRAYER
with Sincere Motive

Prayer is a sincere, sensible, affectionate pouring out of the heart or soul to God, through Christ, in the strength and assistance of the Holy Spirit, for such things as God promised, or according to the Word of God, for the good of the Church, with submission in faith to the will of God.
-John Bunyan, Bedford Prison (1662)[1]

Such was the definition of prayer by a man who was imprisoned for unlicensed preaching in Bedford, England. He knew in prison that the only prayer that works is a sincere one. It must be a real prayer for a real need. That definition tells us why some prayers do not get heaven's attention. Yet, men and women still ask.

YOU ASK AND RECEIVE NOT

Man has always been full of needs; hence, he keeps asking. Whether rightfully or otherwise, he cares less. All he wants is to see his needs supplied. Is it wrong to ask? No. We are commanded from the Scriptures to ask and we are further told that we shall receive. But in this case he does not receive. Why? Because he asks amiss—with a wrong motive.

The New Living Translation of James 4:3 tells it in a simpler way. It reads, "Even when you ask, you don't get it because your motives are all wrong—you want only what will give you pleasure."

Motive is crucial to the subject of prayer. Why do you spend so much time in prayer? Is it to consume the answers upon your lust? Have you ever heard some people pray to God for what they do not *really* need? Oh, they pray with fervency and God in His wisdom never gives a look at such a fellow.

Countless people gather and pray to be anointed, but God would not anoint such a soul, why? Their motive is wrong. If God would not anoint Simon the sorcerer but require that his heart be made right with Him, how do you then think He would anoint you if your heart is not right with Him?

Many times we pray, "Oh God bless me," but He knows that if He blesses us, we would consume it upon our lustful desires. And if, by His grace, He does release a bit of blessing, we often go about bragging. Pride sets in and a fall is inevitable. Maybe the reason He has not given us what we have been asking for is because He already knows we would not give Him glory for it, and we would not use it as a source of benefit to others. So why would He bless us?

Perhaps you are praying for a car, a house, or a job. Are you praying sincerely with holy motives? Or are you praying so that when the answer comes, you see yourself as superior to others? If the latter, that kind of prayer life is an empty life. The prayer that works is that which is said with genuineness of need and in alignment with the Word of God. We need to get our priorities right.

The storehouse of heaven is full, but we can only be partakers of such blessings if our quest is real. In his role of psalmist, David helps us to see what real prayer is like.

THE PRAYER OF A PSALMIST'S HEART

David, among others, knew how to relate with God. He said in Psalm 17:1, *"Hear the right, O LORD, attend unto my cry, give ear unto my prayer, that goeth not out of feigned lips."* If there is anything that constantly challenges me in the life of David, it is always his sincere attitude. He calls a spade a spade. He names it like it is.

Look into Psalm 51 and you will see sincerity. Though he was a man full of faults, he knew them and called them by their names before God, in confession. And God was able to use him far above many of his fellows. Little wonder he was able to see so far ahead. Though he was a king, he operated in both the priesthood and the prophetic ministries. The secret of the Lord is indeed with them that fear Him. And to fear Him is to deal sincerely with Him.

As this chapter comes to a close, let's quickly contrast the life of David with that of Ananias and Sapphira in Acts chapter 5. This couple—Ananias and Sapphira—

died because of insincere motives and unrighteousness (they had concealed sin). David's petitions, on the other hand, were answered by God; he received a pardon because he did not conceal his sin but travailed to God for mercy. Beloved to be sincere with God is for your own benefit as every act of insincerity will at some point lead to death.

*The things of God knoweth no man,
but the Spirit of God.*

~ 1 Corinthians 2:11

6

The PRAYER
in the Spirit

*The things of God knoweth no man,
but the Spirit of God.*

~ *1 Corinthians 2:11*

When Christ announced His departure to His disciples, it caused them great grief. But the Master reasoned with them that they needed to be happy about his leaving because if He didn't go, the Father's work would be limited—the Comforter would not come. He told them that the Spirit of truth would not be released if He did not go; and when the Holy Spirit of truth comes, He would bring with Him a whole lot of benefits. Praying in the Spirit was one of these essential benefits. We are able to pray successfully with the aid of the Spirit. And we pray according to the will of God by the help of the Spirit.

It is not enough to do that which is good; praying is good, but it must be done well. Hence, to do justice to praying, it must be said with the help of the Spirit else we labour in vain. There is no true prayer without the Holy Spirit. Every Old Testament personality who prayed effectively did so with the anointing or covering of the Holy Spirit. We will pray amiss when we try to pray without His help. The right words will not come and we will certainly miss our target. However, the Holy Spirit is ever ready to help us pray rightly if we humbly ask for His help. He is our ever-present assistant in the time of need. He is not of such a spirit that compels. He is gentle and will guide us if He has our approval.

When some people hear the phrase *praying in the spirit*, what comes into their mind is praying in tongues (an unknown language). They are not totally wrong. When we use the phrase *praying in the spirit*, we could be saying *praying in an unknown language*, but we could also be saying, *praying under the inspiration of the Holy Spirit*, or *uttering words that are divinely inspired*, or *praying with the help of the Holy Spirit*.

Likewise when these forms of prayers are in process, one could pray in a language he does understand and without prior notice of what his prayer is concerning. Also one could as well pray in a language that he does not understand but perhaps others around him do understand. Or he could pray in a language that he does understand and others around him may not understand. Finally, he could pray in a language that only God understands.

To pray in the Spirit is to be more conscious of spiritual things than your physical environment. It is

The Prayer *in the Spirit*

the realm where time does not matter. Three hours with God seem like five minutes. This is what the old fathers of faith called, "Lost in His presence" or "Lost in the Spirit." It is a realm in which you do not care a bit about anything natural. You are lost in the supernatural.

However, for the purpose of this book, we shall narrow our focus to praying in unknown languages as an aspect of praying in the Spirit and the necessity of praying in the Spirit with regards to praying in tongues.

WEAKNESS IN PRAYER

The [Holy] Spirit also helpeth our infirmities [weakness]: for we know not what we should pray for as we ought: but the Spirit itself maketh intercession for us with groanings which cannot be uttered (Rom. 8:26).

A believer comes in contact with many challenges throughout his walk toward Christ. He knows the Bible requires that he pray. He knows that if he is going to prevail in his affairs, he *must* pray. He knows that he must pray to the Father in the name of the Son. But to what extent is he required to pray? That he does not know. He is helpless in knowing without the Spirit.

Some believers think they know their needs and how to get their needs met; hence, they go on to ask for things but never receive answers. It is not enough to know what our needs are; we must also know how to get them met. Bringing Scriptural truths into con-

The Prayer *That Works*

sideration, we often don't really and deeply know what our needs are.

For example, a man named E. A. Adeboye, who had been called into full-time ministry, was praying to God for a better accommodation to live in. Day-to-day living was challenging for him after leaving the good pay of a full-time job. But he answered the divine call even without certainty of income. So he prayed and, as he continued to pray, the Lord said to him, "You are asking me for a room, but I have decided to give you a city." Today, "Redemption Camp" of the Redeemed Christian Church of God is a city of its own and Pastor **E. A. Adeboye is its General Overseer.**[1] I don't know about you, but I would desire a city and not just a room.

Pastor Adeboye's initial prayer contained a serious weaknesses, which we all make. He really did need a better accommodation but asking for a room just to get by was the weakness. The Spirit helped his weakness by changing his focus and as a result he was able to pray correctly.

Soul winners often pray with weakness, too. They might pray to win a soul a day, but if the soul winner would pray in the Spirit, he might win ten a day. That is how limited our human minds can be compared to the infinite wisdom of God.

The Spirit says, "There is no real prayer without Me. And if I am absent, the answers will not come." Comprehension of this fact will save us a lot of time and lost opportunities for the kingdom.

REAL PRAYER

Real prayer cannot be uttered with the carnal mind. *"But the Spirit Itself maketh intercession for us with groanings which cannot be uttered"* (Romans 8:26). We can also say it like this, "The Spirit speaks forth those words which are too deep, too painful, and too many for human expression." Hence, if prayer must work, then it must be by the Spirit. It is the Spirit that gives life. Relying on any other effort, the actualization of our needs will prove futile.

A wonderful illustration of praying in the power of the Spirit was told by a pastor in one of his sermons. He said that one day, as he sat praying over the prayer requests from his partners in the ministry, he suddenly felt an awesome presence. Our Lord appeared. He called the brother's name and said to him, "I have come to pray together with you on these requests." As they both knelt down and laid hands on these requests, he said he took special note of how our Lord prayed.

The brother expected loud, discernable words to come out of our Lord's mouth. To his surprise, he found that our Lord did not utter any word. He just laid hands on the paper, looked towards heaven, and sighed. After a while the Lord said to him, *"It has been granted, bring the next one."* The brother was amazed. That was how he and the Lord prayed on every one of those requests. Our Lord showed him a new dimension of prayer.

The topic of praying in the Spirit also reminds me of the story in Mark 7:32-33 of a deaf man with a speech impediment that our Lord prayed for: *"[The people] beseech [Jesus] to put his hand upon him. And he took him aside from the multitude, and put his fingers into his ears, and he spit, and touched his tongue"* (AMP).

Verses 34 and 35 say, *"**And looking up to heaven, he sighed**, and saith unto him, **Ephphatha, that is, Be opened**. And straightway [immediately] his ears were opened, and the string of his tongue was loosed, and he spake plain"* (AMP).

What a glorious deliverance our Lord did, with the help of the Holy Spirit. Though Christ spoke in a known language, his prayer was Spirit-driven and inspired, for "The Lord is the Spirit, and where the Spirit of the Lord is, there is freedom" (2 Cor. 3:17).

THE THINGS OF THE SPIRIT KNOWS NO MAN: UNVEILING SPIRITUAL MYSTERIES

A mystery is something you might not be able to see, but you undoubtedly feel its effect. It cannot be thrown away or denied. Take air for instance. We can't really see it, but we have proof that it is with us.

Likewise, as believers, we are bombarded with spiritual challenges we cannot see. The apostle Paul gave us many pictures of these spiritual forces. He said that we wrestle against *"despotisms, against the powers, against [the master spirits who are] the world rulers of this present darkness, against the spirit forces of wickedness in the heavenly (supernatural) sphere"* (Eph. 6:12 AMP).

How do we deal with these spiritual forces of darkness? Paul gives us the answer. In Ephesians chapter 6, he says, *"Lift up over all the [covering] shield of saving faith, upon which you can quench all the flaming missiles of the wicked [one]. And take the helmet of salvation and the sword that the Spirit wields, which is the word of God. **Pray at all times** [on every occa-*

sion, in every season] ***in the Spirit, with all [manner of] prayer and entreaty.*** *To that end keep alert and watch with strong purpose and perseverance, interceding in behalf of all the saints* [God's consecrated people]" (Eph. 16-18 AMP).

The art of praying in the Spirit is not of man; it is of God and no man can understand it. When you experience it, you may not be able to explain it but you know it works. I remember, an incident, when I was driving and suddenly I began praying in the Spirit (praying in tongues) as I approached a turn. Without looking properly, I proceeded not knowing a car was coming toward me. The driver had to swerve to avoid hitting me. Considering his speed, it would have been a fatal accident had we collided, but glory to God who hasn't left His children defenceless!

Another mysterious aspect of praying in the Spirit is the ability to pray for all the saints. We are able to *"keep alert and watch with strong purpose and perseverance, interceding in behalf of all the saints (God's consecrated people)"* (Eph. 6:18 AMP). I do not know all the saints, but the Holy Spirit does. So as I engage Him in praying, He unveils to me any of the saints that need to be interceded for, and I am able to pray for them effectively with His help.

So often when I pray in the Spirit, the Holy Spirit will stamp a picture of a friend or relative on my heart with a specific word for him or her. Whenever I am able to pass across the message to them, their testimony often bear witness with the word I received from the Spirit. So many lives have been touched.

For example, I had not heard from a friend of mine, whom I will call brother Frank, in a long time.

As I was before the Lord one day, brother Frank was stamped—so to speak—on my heart, and the word of the Lord came to me from 1 Corinthians 2:5: "Your faith should not stand in the wisdom of men, but in the power of God." I did not understand what this word meant as it wasn't for me, but I obeyed the Lord and got in touch with brother Frank through e-mail and I left it at that. Few month down the line, I met him at a conference and we renewed acquaintances. He then began to appreciate the word the Lord had given me. He said, he had lost his job. He also had challenges with his immigration status and his relationship with his girlfriend fell apart. All these happened to him in a short space of time and at that point, he got the word I had sent him. Thank God we serve a God who cares.

Another time, while praying before the Lord, I suddenly knew about an impending event in a brother's life, a man who is a beloved friend in the faith. I met with him and said, "I saw you leave but before you go make sure you get the blessing of the father of the house." His reaction proved these words were indeed from the Lord to him. To prove that what I had said to him was indeed from the Lord, he showed me some personal prophecies which were in line with what I had said to him and some other plans the Lord has for him.

Thousands, perhaps millions, of people have interceded successfully for missionaries with the aid of the Spirit without having prior knowledge of any challenges they may be facing on the mission field. For instance, I read of missionaries who were about to be killed by native country men, but someone back home was interceding in the Spirit for these endangered souls. As the native men approached the missionary's house to carry out the murder, they could not enter. They said they saw a giant man with a shinning sword standing at the entrance of their house. Cases like these are unending.

THE MINISTRY OF THE SPIRIT

John G. Lake rightly said, "The ministry of the Christian is the ministry of the *Spirit*. If the Christian cannot minister the Spirit of God in the true—real—sense, he is not a Christian. If he has not the Spirit to minister in the real high sense, he has nothing to minister. Other men have intellectuality, but the Christian is supposed to be the possessor of the Spirit"[2] This great man of God sees all Christians as a minister, but we often do not see ourselves like that. Oh, how irresponsible we are.

There are many aspects of the Spirit as it pertains to us as believers, and His ministry to and through us. But we are in the subject of prayer, and so we shall consider more on His ministry in us through prayer.

Peter was a weakling at the altar of prayer before the day of Pentecost. He could not go all the way with the Lord; he could only go as far as his mental and physical ability allowed him. He denied the Master because by his own strength shall no man prevail. Real success comes by the help of the Spirit. After Jesus died, the apostles had nothing to do, no power to minister to anyone about anything; hence, they went back to their respective businesses. Peter went back to fishing. Matthew probably went back to the tax office and resumed his duties. But God be blessed forevermore. He went after his disciples and gave them the real thing—the incredible ability to minister in the power of the Holy Spirit. Thus, after the filling of the Holy Spirit in Acts 2, we see Peter—a former weakling—now a prayer champion.

THE LANGUAGE OF THE SPIRIT

The Spirit has a language, a heavenly language, a mysterious language unknown to man but known to God the Father of spirits (1 Cor. 14:2). Speaking this language requires a baptism as described in the book of Acts chapter 2.

A man of God was asked about the success of his ministry and all he had to say was, "Praying in tongues is the making of my ministry; it is that peculiar communication with God when God reveals to my soul the truth I utter to you day by day in the ministry."[3] John G. Lake was known for his boldness and faith. It was said of him that he knew how to choose his words carefully. He had a right word of expression in every situation.

Paul, the apostle, also knew very well about this aspect of the ministry of the Spirit. He made maximum use of it. Little wonder at the magnitude of his results. Paul was a man of revelation and deep wisdom. He said at some point that he prayed in tongues—the Spirit's language—more than the whole Church in Corinth (1 Cor. 14:18). That is incredible.

Do you wonder why he wrote almost the whole of the New Testament or why he could write such deep revelations about "grace" though he was not among the disciples while Christ was alive? A minister friend once commented to me, "I do not cease to be amazed

The Prayer *in the Spirit*

at the exploits of Paul who got saved several years after Christ had left, whereas many of the twelve who walked, talked and ate with Him never made much impact." The answer is found in Paul's determination of knowing Christ alone, and the real source of knowing Christ is through the Holy Spirit. When the Holy Spirit is engaged through speaking in tongues, God is magnified and Christ is revealed.

Knowing all this about Paul we don't need to wonder how he had such great conversions among the gentiles. He understood the kind of prayer that works—praying in the Spirit. He said to the Galatian Church. *"My little children, of whom I **travail in birth** again until Christ be formed in you"* (Gal. 4:19). This aspect of the ministry of the Spirit has been fought greatly by the pit of hell and the reason behind it is simple. We achieve more and we achieve it faster when we pray in tongues. We cut him—the devil—out of the communication line when we pray in an unknown tongue. First Corinthians chapter 14 verse 2 reads, *"For he that speaketh in an unknown tongue speaketh not unto men, but unto God: for no man understandeth him; howbeit in the spirit he speaketh mysteries."*

I like to say this verse in this way: "He who prays in tongues, speaks not unto men neither the devil, but unto God: for no man, nor the devil, understands what he is praying for; however, in the Spirit—the realm of God where God Himself is, where He resides—he speaks mysteries that confuse and put the devil to shame!"

Let me illustrate this verse with an example. Once, a minister's wife was involved in a motor accident. When her husband heard the news, he immediately began confessing the word of God and speaking in faith. After two minutes, some strange thoughts flooded his mind telling him, "Your wife will die." He would bind these thoughts, make more faith confessions, again the thoughts would come back. He was a Spirit-filled minister, so he switched from the known to the unknown by praying in the Holy Ghost.

As he prayed, he saw two strange beings, one on each of his shoulders. He knew by revelation those were the demonic spirits speaking to him. So he continued in speaking in tongues and suddenly the demons said to each other, "Do you know what he is saying?" They both replied, "No." Afterwards one said, "I am feeling some heat here, are you?" The other replied, "Yes, I am" and they both said, "We better run." Immediately, they ran away. His wife was miraculously healed from the injuries sustained in the accident.

IN THE SPIRIT, WE CANNOT PRAY AMISS

Due to the weaknesses of the flesh, our prayer requests are sometimes selfish. When we pray in our own understanding (native language), we are tempted to be "me focused." Our requests might sound like this: "Oh dear Lord, bless me, my mother, father, wife, son, daughter." The subject is always, "me" and "my." We can rest assured that all self-centered requests are cut off when we pray in the Spirit. We can count on Him that He is praying in us, through us, and perhaps for us in our real need for the hour.

The longer we spend praying in the Spirit the better. We will hit a gusher if we pray long enough; the mind of the Spirit concerning our destiny will be unfolded.

Many of us know the *what* of our destiny, but few know the *how*. To ride on the wings of divine fulfilment, we need to know both and walk accordingly. Praying in the Spirit will not only tell us the *what* it will also reveal the *how*. *You see, there could be a specific call or assignment from God upon you, not necessarily into the ministry. You may even know what that call is, but how do you go about fulfilling it God's way? You may not know, but when you depend on the Holy Spirit, He will lead you in the way.*

THE JUST SHALL LIVE BY FAITH

New Testament prayer is prayer purely by faith. Anything done without faith is sin. The kingdom of God works by faith. Without faith, we cannot please the Father. When we pray in tongues—our understanding is unfruitful. We do not know what we are speaking except by interpretation. We can interpret if we desire by the enablement of the Holy Spirit through our prayers. 1 Corinthians 14:13 says, *"The person who speaks in an [unknown] tongue should pray [for the power] to interpret and explain what he says"* (Amp).

Praying in the Spirit requires faith, but more importantly it builds up our faith. We are able to believe God for something very extraordinary. The supernatural becomes natural. Brother Jude spoke along this line in his 20th verse: *"Beloved, building up yourselves on your most holy faith, praying in the Holy Ghost."* Now, I want you to see something. Brother Jude is saying, "Brother Ayodeji, build up yourself on your most holy faith." And I answer, "How can I do that?" And he replies, "By praying in the Holy Ghost."

I believe that by this method of praying, every form of unbelief can be dealt with. The Amplified version of this particular verse puts it this way, *"But you, beloved, build yourselves up [founded] on your most holy faith [make progress, rise like an edifice higher and higher], praying in the Holy Spirit."* Sadly, many have fallen because of unbelief. But let me assure you, dear reader, that if you pray in the Spirit long enough, you will experience a tremendous change in your walk with the Lord. You will no longer pray amiss—you will pray the very mind of God for your life. Divine agenda will unfold before your eyes

CAN I PRAY WITHOUT THE SPIRIT'S BAPTISM?

"Brother Ayodeji, can I pray without the baptism of the Spirit?" You may be wondering. Yes, you can. But I believe that you won't be able to pray effectively. You may say, "I'm not baptized, but I pray and I get results." Understand that the results you get cannot be compared with what you would get if you were baptized in the Spirit.

I hear you reply, "Were the Old Testament saints baptized?" Study your Bible very well; everyone that accomplished great things for God had the Spirit upon them, though they never spoke in tongues. Speaking in tongues is a New Testament phenomenon. It belongs to us under the new covenant.

There is a great need for the baptism in the Holy Ghost with the evidence of speaking with tongues. It is so essential. You must be hungry for it. Inasmuch as you must drink water after your meal, then you must be baptized in the Spirit.

Let me share something here to further illustrate the need for the Spirit. "Cultivating Your Friendship with the Holy Spirit," was the title of the message shared one day by a pastor who stressed that to keep a vibrant relationship with the Spirit, we must be able to speak in the language of the Spirit. Afterwards, during the announcements the announcer said, "If you are not baptized in the Holy Ghost with the evidence of speaking in tongues do not go home, it is very dangerous to leave without the Spirit's baptism." People gathered after the service, they were told of what to expect and almost all were baptized in the Holy Ghost with evidence of the heavenly language.

For further study on praying in the Spirit, I recommend these two books that have led me into a deeper, more effectual prayer life: *Tongues: Beyond The Upper Room* by Kenneth E. Hagin and *The Walk Of The Spirit—The Walk Of Power* by Dave Roberson.

Ye have not chosen me, but I have chosen you, and ordained you, that ye should go and bring forth fruit, and that your fruit should remain: that whatsoever ye shall ask of the Father in my name, he may give it you.

~ John 15:16

7

The PRAYER
of a Soul Winner

Ye have not chosen me, but I have chosen you, and ordained you, that ye should go and bring forth fruit, and that your fruit should remain: that whatsoever ye shall ask of the Father in my name, he may give it you.

~ John 15:16

God is greatly and desperately in need. Unfortunately, few among us see His need or set aside time to discover His need. Frankly, this attitude stinks in His nostrils. This is the hard fact. Selfishness is foolishness in the Father's sight. It takes a spiritual man to discern the need of God.

The apostles could not discern the need of the Father, but the Son could. He said to them, *"My meat is to do the will of him that sent me, and to finish his work. Say not ye, There are yet four months, and then cometh harvest? behold, I say unto you, Lift up your eyes, and look on the fields; for they are white already to harvest"* (John 4:34-35). The Son knew very well the need of the Father and he went where that need could be met.

This is why when Jesus was on his way to Galilee, we are told, *"He **must needs** go through Samaria"* (John 4:4). Why must He? There were better routes to His destination, but because He knew that a soul would be there, at the well, and because she must be saved, He had no choice but to travel through the land of Samaria.

HE THAT IS SPIRITUAL

I want to focus our thoughts now on the sharp and deep phrase, "He that is Spiritual." We could say in our common language, "Someone with great acumen." The New Living Translation says, "Those who are Spiritual." From this passage, it is evident that not every one of us is spiritual. Not every one of us is consciously mindful of spiritual things.

Not all of us give ourselves to the things of God. To know that we are not all spiritual, all we have to do is compare our dedication to godly things to that of worldly things. All we have to do is check the level of worldliness in the Church. All we have to do is check how we treat one another. All we have to do is—if granted by God—listen to our hearts, what goes on in there.

For instance, I have heard some people talk about their pastor in a manner that is not Scriptural. Such people cannot be blessed by that vessel (the pastor). And while the sermon is preached in church, begging them to serve God, some people's minds are far off. Oh, how far away we have gone. We hear sermons but leave with no commensurate repentance. The world cannot distinguish us believers from every other infidel. Is it meant to be like this? Is God pleased with your spirituality? How spiritual are you?

Where Are They?

A minister of the gospel preached a sermon. He started with this question I would like to throw to you, "Where can you find a spiritual person?" Almost the whole congregation said, "Church." The preacher said "No," and went ahead to tell the congregation the answer, which I believe is perfectly right. He said you would find a spiritual person at home. Not in churches. What we have nowadays in churches are artists. A majority make up a show of holiness whereas wickedness is inside. I'll add that he who is spiritual is a consistent man wherever you put him.

God's Greatest Need

We have established that God has needs, and man is also an entity of need. John 10:10 gives an excellent picture of the need of man. Jesus said, *"I am come that they (Man) might have life, and that they might have it more abundantly."* The greatest need of man is God Himself—the life of God in his being. All other needs (though they may be essential) are not as crucial as this life of God. This is the *zoe* life described further on page 109.

Would it not be absurd for Christ to die just to make a man have a good job or be healed or have a good spouse? Certainly it would, but blessed be God that Christ died so as to open the kingdom of God and His righteousness to us and after which every other thing are added to us (Matt. 6:33).

Now, God's greatest need is man. The Scriptures is full of instances where we see God looking for man. In Genesis 3:9, God said, "Adam where art thou." He came down to find man. He also said to Cain, "Where is Abel thy brother?" (Gen. 4:9). The Gospels also confirm that "the Son of Man has come to seek and to save that which was lost" (Luke 19:10, also Matt. 18:11). This has always been the mode of operation with God concerning man. He seeks to find him.

God needs us- man, but we do not seem to know this. The Father sent the only Son not because of goats and dogs. Neither was it because of our great buildings. No! The Son came solely for the sake of man to save him.

Man is so dear to God.

MAN: AN INCREDIBLE BEING

Everything God created was good, but man was said to be very good (Gen. 1:31). Man was given dominion over every other creation of God, and he was blessed with tremendous abilities. That is why we are not amazed at the discoveries made by man over the millennia. In fact, it would be troubling if he hadn't made such findings.

The contribution of man in science and technology, art and media is extremely great. Truly, he has a spirit in him and the inspiration of the Almighty gives him understanding. However, having seen the incredibility of man, we have also established that with all of his endowments, he is still in need of the life of God.

TWO DIMENSIONAL OPERATIONS

Man has two great capacities. First, he has the capacity to *receive* God. He has the supernatural enablement to receive Christ into his being. John 1:12 says, *"But as many **as received him (Jesus Christ),** to them gave he power to become the sons of God."* When man receives Jesus Christ into his being, he receives the ability to become a son of God.

Second, beyond this first ability to receive Christ, he also has a tremendous ability to *reveal* the Christ which he has received. Paul the apostle said, *"When it pleased God, who separated me from my mother's womb, and called me by his grace, to **reveal** his Son in me, that I might preach him among the heathen"* (Gal. 1:15-16). Paul was separated from his people so that he might *reveal* the Christ whom he had received. Paul received so much of God that handkerchiefs were taken from his body to heal the sick. He also revealed so much of God by preaching Christ among the gentiles that several churches were started throughout Asia Minor.

The main purpose of us receiving Christ is to reveal—preach and demonstrate—Him among fellow men, most importantly among the unsaved. This is time-consuming and involves a great deal of responsibilities. To run away from such responsibilities is to disobey the heavenly vision. We are not saved to warm pews. We are saved to be saviours—to be the avenue through which others are brought to the knowledge of the saving grace of Christ. How will they believe if there is no preacher? There are numerous preachers, but what and to whom are they preaching? Perhaps they preach to make their pockets full; their god is their belly and their end is according to their works—destruction!

Countless souls are perishing in hell and some preacher stands behind the pulpit to deceive God's people. Preacher, does your congregation know about hell? Have they been truly blood-washed? Sanctified? And ready to meet their God? Or is the blind leading the blind? Why not have a change of heart and repent? Perhaps God will hear and forgive you.

Precious saints, now is the time to awake out of sleep—spiritual lethargy, slumber and decay. Now is the hour of salvation. Let us cast off every work of darkness and let us put on the armour of light. We are the light of the world. Men are walking in darkness; they need the revelation of our light. What benefit is light to darkness if the light would not go into the darkness and lighten it up? Isaiah 9 verse 2 must be continually fulfilled through us: *"The people that walked in darkness have seen a great light: they that dwell in the land of the shadow of death, upon them hath the light shined."*

WHOSE BUSINESS?

According to spiritual order, God would not come down and preach the gospel; neither would any angel do it. If an angel does it, it will be a breach of divine plan. The command, "Go ye into the world . . . " was given to man not angels. It is man's business to preach the gospel and God's to confirm what has been preached.

Do you wonder why the angel that appeared to Cornelius In Acts 10 would not preach to him but, instead, asked him to call for Peter? Do you think the angel did not know what to say? I'm sure he did know, but if he preached to Cornelius, he would be overstepping his boundary. It is for man to preach to man. God uses man to reach man.

Do you remember the song, "These Are the Days of Elijah"? It says that "out of Zion's hill salvation comes." We are Zion—the New Testament Church—through whom salvation comes. The Book of Romans Chapter 10 verse 12 to 17 confirms the divine pattern:

> *For whosoever shall call upon the name of the Lord shall be saved. How then shall they call on him in whom they have not believed?* ***and how shall they believe in him of whom they have not heard? and how shall they hear without a preacher?*** *And how shall they preach, except they be sent? as it is written, How beautiful are the feet of them that preach the gospel of peace, and bring glad tidings of good things! But they have not all obeyed the gospel. For Esaias saith, Lord, who hath believed our report?* ***So then faith cometh by hearing, and hearing by the word of God.***

How would the faith to believe come? By hearing from a God-sent preacher!

MY FRUITS MUST REMAIN

We are not only called to bear fruits (win souls) but, more importantly, we are commanded to let the souls remain. In John 15:16, Jesus said, *"You have not chosen me, but I have chosen you, and ordained you, that you should go and bring forth fruit, and that your fruit should remain: that whatsoever you shall ask of the Father in my name, he may give it to you."*

We are given whatever we ask for because the fruit remains—not because we bore the fruits, though it is a great thing to bear fruits. There is no limit to what we can ask for if the souls remain. *Whatsoever* means *whatsoever*. It means *anything*. There is no quota as long as it's in the confines of God's will and centered on glorifying Him, then whatever we ask will be given to us. What a great privilege a real, ardent soul winner enjoys!

However, what would you call a fisherman who catches fish in the hundreds and puts them back into the sea? That would be a great waste of resources. Hence, we are warned against such practices, too. There is a great tendency to fall into such error on our path to soul winning perhaps due to laziness, negligence of duty, and inadequate knowledge.

We must, therefore, be careful not to engage in profitless labour. We should endeavour to acquire those things which will make the souls remain. I must establish that every soul that remains is according to His will because He works in the souls to will and to do. However, our input cannot be put off; He works through us for the benefit of new souls. This is where rigorous follow up is essential. Placing the soul in a Bible-believing and teaching church and praying for them until Christ is formed in them are our responsibilities. Without this sort of plan, winning souls would be wasted time.

HE SEES LIKE THE FATHER

A man with a heart for fruit that remains sees the same way the Father sees. He knows the heartbeat of the Father. He can see the burden of the Father. The zeal of the house of the Father has consumed him. What concerns God naturally concerns him. Do you now think that such a man would ask anything of the Father and it would not be done?

Are you surprised that Jesus' requests were all granted? The Son said that he must finish the work of Him that sent him. What then is the work of Him that sent him? Preaching the gospel of the kingdom and going after the lost sheep wherever He could find them. The Son was a great soul winner!

Are you also surprised that God could not do anything against the land of Sodom and Gomorrah without telling Abraham? The man Abraham was a great intercessor, a soul deliverer (Gen. 14, 18:17-19).

Are you surprised at the depth of Paul's spiritual knowledge? All you need to do is read his epistles to the churches and the Acts of the Apostles and you will no longer be. If we all were as zealous for souls as Paul was, then we would be turning sinners to Christ in a greater dimension. And it is also a fact that a prayer that works is a prayer by one who is zealous for souls.

I heard about a great man of God who never seemed to pray long enough in public to satisfy people. They forgot that most prayers of the saints said publicly were very short. Even Christ seldom prayed long publicly. The only exception to this was His great prayer in the book of John, chapter 17. Public prayers need not be long, but private prayer should be long if we desire to avail much. However, even the short prayers of this godly man were often answered.

This caused a bit of wonder and concern among the people, until the man discovered the secret behind those prayers which were answered: the more time he spent fellowshipping with the Holy Spirit and winning souls to the kingdom, the more his requests were answered.

Beloved, that is the key. When we see like He sees, He does not withhold anything from us. No good thing will He withhold from them that do His bidding (soul winning). He who wins souls is wise. He is selfless. He is all out for God, and he that goes all out for God has all of God at his disposal. He carries a great and heavy spiritual authority.

FATHER NASH

During Charles G. Finney's revivals, there was a man named Father Nash who worked with him—a man of prayer that saw the way God sees. Father Nash loved souls so much that he would go weeks ahead of Finney to the location of the next revival to prepare for the event with fervent prayers. It was also said that Nash carried a great anointing and authority that Finney acknowledged.

A story is told that that one time as they prepared for the next revival, a group of boys in the area approached Finney and made it known to him that they would resist the revival. Finney called Nash's attention to it and both went into a grove of trees and prayed until they felt they had gained the victory. Nash then sought for an audience with the young men and he boldly told them toward the end of the meeting that God would break their ranks in less than one week either by converting some of them or sending some of them to hell. He said it with all assurance.

Finney feared when he heard of Nash's verdict. By the end of the week all the young men were saved. Some of them actually came back crying and asking Finney what they ought to do in order to be saved.[1]

Oh how great an authority the Church has at her disposal. Does she use it? She would get a greater result if she has the full revelation of the authority at her disposal.

In soul winning, God is glorified and there is great joy in heaven over every soul that repents. Each of us can be a source of joy to heaven.

The earnest (heartfelt, continued) prayer of a righteous man makes tremendous power available [dynamic in its working].

~ James 5:16 (AMP)

8

The
PRAYER
That Is Continuous

The earnest (heartfelt, continued) prayer of a righteous man makes tremendous power available [dynamic in its working]
~ James 5:16 (AMP)

Let us consider again the story of Elijah as recorded in 1 Kings 18:43-45. Previously we dealt with his fervency (v. 42). Now we shall explore his *continuous persistence* or, rather, his *importunity* in prayer.

We must realize that importunity is essential to successful praying. Although many have taught otherwise, preachers and teachers of the word of God say that persistent prayer is an act of unbelief; we cannot get anymore unscriptural than that. However, their teaching is not supported in the Scripture. Elijah, for example, knew the art of praying successfully. He had the tenacity to prevail with God in prayer. It takes importunity to prevail with God.

1 Kings 18:43-45

[Elijah] said to his servant, Go up now, look toward the sea. And he went up, and looked, and said, There is nothing. And he said, Go again seven times. And it came to pass at the seventh time, that he said, Behold, there ariseth a little cloud out of the sea, like a man's hand. And he said, Go up, say unto Ahab, Prepare thy chariot, and get thee down that the rain stop thee not. And it came to pass in the mean while, that the heaven was black with clouds and wind, and there was a great rain. And Ahab rode, and went to Jezreel. The hand of the Lord was on Elijah; and he girded up his loins, and ran before Ahab to the entrance of Jezreel.

Elijah was able to see the realization of God's promises due to his importunity. Tarrying with God is not an act of unbelief. On the contrary, importunity is an act of faith and absolute trust in God. Looking closely at the life of Elijah and his great achievements, it takes great faith to do what he did. It takes a man of faith to call down fire; he called it thrice. It takes faith to raise the dead; he raised one. (In fact, he stretched upon the child *three* times before the boy came back to life.) It takes great faith to be taken into heaven; he was caught into heaven by chariots of fire.

Everything Elijah did was out of utter belief in Jehovah, his God. He knew he had to pray until his joy was full. The same was true for his successor Elisha. To save Naaman from leprosy, Elisha instructed him to wash himself seven times in the river. Naaman didn't just have to wash himself in the river; he had to continue until the seventh time. His deliverance was attached not to the first time but the seventh! (See 2 Kings 5:1-14.)

Beloved, you do not know what hour your deliverance is attached to, so it is wisdom to continue. There is a light at the end of the tunnel.

Jacob was another man who prevailed with God because he was importunate. He would not let God go until he was blessed; he would not stop until something tangible happened. (See Genesis 32:22-32.)

DANIEL THE PROPHET

Though in the midst of oppression, captivity, unfriendly friends, and demonic laws, Daniel knew he had to pray and pray some more until something happened. He understood the dynamics of prayer; he knew that God wasn't a taskmaster but that there were forces of darkness he had to deal with in prayers. He used a philosophy some of us use today: Pray Until Something Happens (Operation P.U.S.H.).

Though he was a very busy man, he never allowed his busyness to debar him from praying continually to his God. The book of Daniel chapter 9 shows us how continually Daniel prayed. It showed us of his importunity at the altar of prayer. There was something that Daniel had; there was something he possessed in his being. It was the supernatural strength to pray through each situation.

The Prayer *That Works*

It is not enough to pray; you must ensure to pray through. And when you do pray through, you will know when you're through.

Among many things, Daniel understood what Paul described in the book of Ephesians chapter 6 verse 12: *"We wrestle not against flesh and blood, but against principalities, against powers, against the rulers of the darkness of this world, against spiritual wickedness in high places."* Daniel knew that he was wrestling with something beyond the physical.

I don't know much about the game of wrestling, but from what I see on television, it seems to be a sport that has little or no rule. It is a game in which two competitors attempt to throw and slam each other by any possible means. It is designed so that you can fight however you wish; you can carry the opponent, slam the fellow on the ground, and be declared the winner by the count of three. This game tells me one thing: it is geared toward immobilization. In fact, there have been many occasions where some wrestlers had to leave the ring with broken bones.

Daniel seemed to realize that if he did not continue steadfastly in prayer he could be immobilized by the forces of darkness. How many saints have been immobilized through their lack of continuity in prayers? They would not pray enough; hence they are defeated in battle. They experience failure at the edge of breakthrough, failure at the edge of total victory. They almost became winners, but now they are losers. They almost got their freedom, but now they are captives of the mighty. They almost got to their promised lands but did not enter because they would not continue steadfastly in prayer.

APOSTOLIC IMPORTUNITY

The early church knew something about this kind of prayer. Though the Holy Ghost was promised, they still had to pray through the issues at hand. It is not enough to receive promises from God; ultimately, it is us who must ensure that those promises are fulfilled, through prayer, as the apostles did.

Acts 1:14

> These **all continued with one accord in prayer** and supplication, with the women, and Mary the mother of Jesus, and with his brethren.

Acts 2:1-4

> *And when the day of Pentecost was fully come, they were all with one accord in one place. And suddenly there came a sound from heaven as of a rushing mighty wind, and it filled all the house where they were sitting. And there appeared unto them cloven tongues like as of fire, and it sat upon each of them. And they were all filled with the Holy Ghost, and began to speak with other tongues, as the Spirit gave them utterance.*

Beloved, what would have happened on the day of Pentecost if the apostles had gotten weary before the big day arrived? What would have happened if Peter had said, "Brethren, we have prayed enough and the Holy Spirit is not here. Let us go"? Would the Holy Spirit have come? How powerless the church would have been without Him. Praise God the apostles practiced the importunity of prayer.

JUST A LITTLE MORE

When Elisha neared the end of his life, the king of Israel visited him seeking counsel on how to be delivered from the Syrians who were on the verge of destroying his kingdom. Elisha gave the king specific instructions for how to defeat Syria, instructions on importunity:

2 Kings 13:14-19

> *Elisha was fallen sick of his sickness And Joash the king of Israel came down unto him, and wept over his face, and said, O my father, my father, the chariot of Israel, and the horsemen thereof.*
> *And Elisha said unto him, Take bow and arrows. And he took unto him bow and arrows. And he said to the king of Israel, Put thine hand upon the bow. And he put his hand upon it: and Elisha put his hands upon the king's hands. And he said, Open the window eastward. And he opened it. Then Elisha said, Shoot. And he shot. And he said, The arrow of the Lord's deliverance, and the arrow of deliverance from Syria: for thou shalt smite the Syrians in Aphek, till thou have consumed them.*
> *And he said, Take the arrows. And he took them. And he said unto the king of Israel, Smite upon the ground. And he smote thrice, and stayed. And the man of God was wroth with him, and said,* **Thou shouldest have smitten five or six times; then hadst thou smitten Syria till thou hadst consumed it: whereas now thou shalt smite Syria but thrice.**

Elisha gave the king of Israel specific instructions for how to defeat Syria, but unfortunately the king didn't fully obey those instructions. He had the hand of Elisha upon him (which signifies the hand of the Lord), but he still could not utterly defeat his enemies.

The Amplified Bible translation tells 2 Kings 13 verse 19 like this, "You should have struck five or six times; then you would have struck down Syria until you had destroyed it. But now you shall strike Syria down only three times." That is the reason why many believers end up with half deliverance. God wants total deliverance for us, but do we want total or half deliverance?

Elisha, in essence, told the king of Israel, "You would have totally destroyed Syria had you continued a bit more, but now your victory shall be short lived." Do you see why it seems like you experience a bit of victory and then defeat? A bit of success and then failure? A bit of abundance and then scarcity? A bit of deliverance and then bondage?

NEW TESTAMENT PRAYER PATTERN

Jesus Christ warned us against vain repetition of words and syllables. Vain repetition is a prayer of unbelief; it is a form of prayer that is fleshly driven and hypocritical. But on the contrary, the continuous prayer of a believer is born out of faith because he knows that faithful is He that has called him, who also will answer him.

Another reason we as the New Testament saints should be importunate in prayer is because this is the laid-down rule by our Master—Jesus Christ Himself.

The Prayer *That Works*

He told the disciples a parable to illustrate the immense benefit of continuous prayer:

Luke 18:1-8 NLT

*One day Jesus told his disciples a story to show that they should always pray and never give up. There was a judge in a certain city," he said, "who neither feared God nor cared about people. A widow of that city came to him repeatedly, saying, 'Give me justice in this dispute with my enemy.' The judge ignored her for a while, but finally he said to himself, 'I don't fear God or care about people, but this woman is driving me crazy. I'm going to see that she gets justice, because she is wearing me out with her constant requests!'" Then the Lord said, **"Learn a lesson from this unjust judge**. Even he rendered a just decision in the end. So don't you think God will surely give justice to his chosen people who cry out to him day and night? Will he keep putting them off? I tell you, he will grant justice to them quickly! But when the Son of Man returns, how many will he find on the earth who have faith?"*

Jesus compared an unjust judge with His heavenly Father. He said, "Learn a lesson from this unjust judge." Though he was unjust we can still learn a lot from him. This tells me something, that no matter how terrible a situation may appear, we can always learn something good from it if we would allow the Spirit to teach us that which we do not know. So what was it that the disciples did not know and they needed to know? It was persistency, perseverance, importunity,

The Prayer *That Is Continuous*

and faith as it pertains to praying. Remember our Lord started by saying, "They (the disciples) should always pray and never give up." That applies to you and me, as well.

The prayer that works is that which is rendered both day and night. *"So don't you think God will surely give justice to his chosen people who cry out to him **day and night**? Will he keep putting them off? I tell you, he will grant justice to them quickly!"* Because we are importunate, God will never put us off. I tell you, He will grant answers to our petition quickly.

To show that importunity is not an act of unbelief as some teach, Jesus ended the parable with a question. He asked, *"But when the Son of Man returns, how many will he **find on the earth who have faith**?"* Jesus is showing us that it takes faith to be importunate. Would you go to a man for help whom you know has no capacity to help you? I would not. I would rather continually go to the one I know who has the capacity to render appropriate help unto me.

It takes faith to take God at His word. He who cannot take God at His word cannot win in the world. May you this day be baptized with the strength from heaven that enables you to prevail in prayer.

*And when **they** had prayed*

~ Acts 4:31

9

The PRAYER
That Is Unified

*And when **they** had prayed*
~ Acts 4:31

This chapter on corporate prayer does not in any way undermine the ministry of personal prayer. I personally believe in private prayer as it has immense benefit to an individual's spiritual growth. In fact, I believe that personal prayer is the wheel that drives corporate prayer. Personal prayer is the lifeline of general prayer. Without a vibrant personal prayer life, corporate praying would not generate the kind of result that it should. Hence, I do believe and practice personal praying, but when I get together with others who practice personal prayer, there is a greater level of achievement.

The Bible is full of instances where corporate praying has proved to be a great success, some of which I shall elaborate on here.

THE BIRTH OF THE NEW TESTAMENT CHURCH

There is something supernatural about corporate praying—it even has the ability to give birth. In chapter 2, I referred to the revival that swept the nation of Argentina—a revival birthed by corporate praying. This should not surprise us, for clearly stated in the Scriptures, corporate praying led to the glorious birth of the New Testament Church as described in the book of Acts chapter 2.

ACTS 2:1-5

> *And when the day of Pentecost was fully come, they were all with one accord in one place. And suddenly there came a sound from heaven as of a rushing mighty wind, and it filled all the house where they were sitting. And there appeared unto them cloven tongues like as of fire, and it sat upon each of them. And they were all filled with the Holy Ghost, and began to speak with other tongues, as the Spirit gave them utterance. And there were dwelling at Jerusalem Jews, devout men, out of every nation under heaven.*

When Jesus appeared to the disciples in Luke chapter 24, verses 36-53, He told them what to do in order to receive the promise of the Father—the Holy Spirit, which invariably gave birth to the Church. Now, in the book of Acts, chapter two, we see how the promise was delivered to the apostles—it was by corporate praying. The New Testament church was birthed by corporate praying. The church today knows little about the purpose and power of corporate praying though we gather together, not for kingdom purposes but rather for selfish purposes.

CORPORATE PRAYING BRINGS DELIVERANCE

Another benefit we derive from corporate praying is deliverance. Two instances in Scripture reveal this. First, in the book of Acts chapter 4, the apostles were threatened by the council of the Sanhedrin not to preach in the name of Jesus (we could say they were *cautioned* not to preach in the name of Jesus). However, the apostles being adamant, refused to bow down to any threat.

Verse 20 states the reply of Peter and John to the council: "For we cannot but speak the things which we have seen and heard." Following this confrontation the apostles were then released and went to their *own company* (v. 23)—thank God they had a company! Do you have a company?

Verses 24 says, "And when *they* heard that, *they* lifted up *their* voice to God with one accord, and said, Lord, thou art God." Take notice of the words "they" and "their," which are plural. The challenge the universal church faces would never be the job of one person if she is going to triumph. The job is for *us* all and *we* must see it that way if we desire to experience our more-than-conqueror heritage.

Now, verse 31 also says, "And when *they* had prayed, the place was shaken where *they* were assembled together; and *they* were all filled with the Holy Ghost, and *they* spake the word of God with boldness." Also take notice of the word "they," which further confirms the blessings derived from corporate praying. They were all filled with the Holy Ghost because they prayed together.

When we read further through the book of Acts, cooperate praying is a vivid thread that weaves through the apostles. They stayed together, prayed together, and God used them mightily together.

The second illustration of deliverance is that of Peter. In Acts chapter 12, we read of how James, the brother of John, had been imprisoned. In the same chapter, we read that James was killed, but Peter was supernaturally delivered. Why did Peter survive? Verse 5 of the same chapter reveals the secret. It says, "Peter therefore was kept in prison: *but prayer was made without ceasing of the church unto God for him.* Prayer from the church—corporate prayer—was ceaselessly made unto the Lord.

When the eyes of our understanding are opened to this dimension of prayer and we turn to God in truth, God will move mightily among us. From these instances, we would see the reason the writer of Hebrews warns us not to forsake the gathering of ourselves. When the body of Christ gathers together, Jesus the head of us all, comes among us to work His wonders. Hence, we read that where two or three are gathered together in His name, there Christ is in their midst.

CALL TO THE MINISTRY CONFIRMED

ACTS 13:2-3

As they ministered to the Lord, and fasted, the Holy Ghost said, Separate me Barnabas and Saul for the work whereunto I have called them. And when they had fasted and prayed, and laid their hands on them, they sent them away.

Apart from deliverance, many other benefits are derived from corporate praying. Acts chapter 13 tells of how Barnabas and Saul of Tarsus (who later became Paul) were called into the ministry by the Holy Spirit—or rather, the Holy Spirit confirmed their ministry. Somewhere in their spirit, something like a *knowing* already alerted them of the call. So when they gathered together, all they heard was just a confirmation.

In most cases, when God is calling someone into a ministry, He first notifies the person—somehow the person knows that there is a call of God upon him. He might not know the full details; however, he has a vague idea about it. If he seeks God more, it becomes clearer.

Be assured, though, that it is dangerous to take aboard a prophecy that you have never picked up in your spirit (so to speak) and run with it. Regardless of who gives it to you. If the prophecy does not bear witness with your spirit, just leave it behind. Even if it is true, if you don't know it in your spirit first, I still advise that you don't run with it. Let God work things out. Be still and see the salvation of the Lord.

I remember when I was in a prophetic meeting. Among many people, a man of God called me out and began telling me things about the call of God upon me. All he said were things I already knew in my spirit by revelation. All he did was confirm it for me. It cancelled out all doubt and established a truth. That is the benefit of corporate prayer meetings. If I had stayed home, I would not have received that confirmation.

MOSES AND HIS COMPANY

The remarkable success Moses experienced in his ministry came about due to many reasons, one of which was corporate praying. One such success is recorded in the book of Exodus.

Exodus 17:8-13

> *Then came Amalek, and fought with Israel in Rephidim. And Moses said unto Joshua, Choose us out men, and go out, fight with Amalek: tomorrow I will stand on the top of the hill with the rod of God in mine hand.*
>
> *So Joshua did as Moses had said to him, and fought with Amalek: and Moses, Aaron, and Hur went up to the top of the hill. And it came to pass, when Moses held up his hand, that Israel prevailed: and when he let down his hand, Amalek prevailed.*
>
> *But Moses hands were heavy; and they took a stone, and put it under him, and he sat thereon; and Aaron and Hur stayed up his hands, the one on the one side, and the other on the other side; and his hands were steady until the going down of the sun. And Joshua discomfited Amalek and his people with the edge of the sword.*

The defeat of Amalek came in totality because of the company of Aaron and Hur—which I shall call his prayer partners—on the battle field. It was not recorded that Moses, Aaron, and Hur engaged in any form of prayers; perhaps they did, but we don't have that account. However, their situation is prophetic in nature—Moses raising up his hands thereby winning battles.

It is also symbolic of the New Testament church because when we pray together, a battle line is immediately drawn between two kingdoms: God's kingdom and Satan's kingdom. In the time of Moses, the children of Israel could be likened to God's kingdom and the Amalekites, Satan's Kingdom. These two kingdoms, regardless of the era, have always been at war.

Moses experienced a measure of success on his own, but he soon got tired. Likewise, we may experience some measure of success on our own, too. But like Moses, we may also get tired. The wisdom, then, is that we should support ourselves with like-minded Aarons and Hurs if we are to experience success in our battles.

DANIEL AND HIS COMPANY

The exploits of Daniel in Babylon—an ungodly nation—is an amazement to anyone that thoroughly would undertake its study. Daniel, like others we have spoken about in this chapter, also had a company: Hananiah—Shadrach; Mishael—Meshach; and Azariah—Abednego.

Daniel's story reveals for us—the New Testament believers—the efficacy of the power that is behind corporate praying. Jesus spoke along this line to His disciples when He made this profound statement, *"If* *two of you shall agree on earth as touching **anything** that they shall ask [as long as it is scriptural], it shall be done for them of my Father which is in heaven. For where two or three are gathered together in my name, there am I in the midst of them"* (Matt. 18:19-20).

Daniel had a problem that he could not solve on his own, so he enlisted the help of his three friends. In the book of Daniel chapter 2, King Nebuchadnezzar had forgotten his dream, so he ordered all the magicians and sorcerers of his kingdom to tell him not only what the dream was but its interpretation. That was a big task for the devil, but not for our God! The king told them he would kill every magician and sorcerer and their families if they could not live up to his expectation—to tell and interpret his dream.

The news caused upheaval in the whole kingdom and somehow it got to Daniel. He approached the king himself because no one could remind the king of his dream, and the king was ready to have them all killed. But Daniel asked the king for some time that he might seek God's face regarding the issue.

Daniel chapter 2:17-19 says, *"Then Daniel went to his house, and made the [matter] known to Hananiah, Mishael, and Azariah, his companions: That they would desire mercies of the God of heaven concerning this secret; that Daniel and his fellows should not perish with the rest of the wise men of Babylon. Then was the secret revealed unto Daniel in a night vision. Then Daniel blessed the God of heaven."*

A Place Called There

From our illustrations of the apostles, Moses, and Daniel, God moves or blesses saints when they come together to pray based on one key element. It is unity! God moves and pours out his blessings when there is unity.

Psalm 133 is a Scripture I love so much and I endeavour to live my life by it: *"Behold, how good and how pleasant it is for brethren to dwell together in unity! It is like the precious ointment upon the head, that ran down upon the beard, even Aaron's beard: that went down to the skirts of his garments; As the dew of Hermon, and as the dew that descended upon the mountains of Zion: for there the LORD commanded the blessing, even life for evermore"* (vv. 1-3).

In other words, disunity quenches the move of the Spirit. The latter part of verse 3 says, *"For there the LORD commanded the blessing, even life for evermore."* The question is, where is "there"? The psalmist, David, says, "for *there* the LORD commanded . . ." The "there" is the place of unity. Unity is the psalmist's emphasis.

The greatest benefit we stand to partake of if we dwell in the place of unity is the life of God, "even *life* for evermore." The Greek word for this eternal life of God is *zoe*, which means having the same order of life as God.

God's order of life is a life of righteousness, peace, and joy (see John 10:10). This blessing of eternal life would minimize the unexplainable tragic death that has befallen some Christians. You see, we have to accept the fact that the opposite of life is death.

What brings death? If unity brings life, invariably disunity—envy and strife—would also produce death.

James spoke along this line when he said, *"For where envying and strife is, there is confusion and every evil work"* (James 3:16). Every evil work includes sickness, disease, infirmity, poverty, lack, frustration, affliction, rejection, depression, suppression, death, and anything evil you can think of.

Therefore, so as not to waste our effort when we gather together for prayer, we must ensure that, individually we are in that place. A place called there. A place called unity.

Prayer of Salvation and Baptism in the Holy Ghost

The will of the Father is that all should come to repentance. The father wants you saved. He sent His only son for that purpose—that tells you how important you are to Him. "For God so loved the world that He gave His only begotten son that whosoever believes in Him should not perish but have everlasting life" (Rom. 3:16).

"For God *so* . . ." The word "so" indicates the intensity and depth of God's love toward you. "That *whosoever believes* . . ." This indicates that anyone can be born again. There is no racial, social, or cultural barrier to God's salvation plan for you. The only thing required of you is to believe in the son whom he sent and you shall be saved. The Scriptures declare that *"if thou shalt confess with thy mouth the Lord Jesus, and shalt believe in thine heart that God hath raised him from the dead, thou shalt be saved. For with the heart man believeth unto righteousness; and with the mouth confession is made unto salvation"* (Rom 10:9-10).

With this understanding, say this prayer with faith in your heart: *Father God, I realize how deep your love is for me and how you demonstrated it by sending your only son to die for me on the cross, whom you raised from the dead. I believe in your son Jesus and all he accomplished by his blood on the cross. Accept me and cleanse me from my sin.*

Having said that prayer from your heart, I believe you are now a child of God. To run this race successfully, you need the baptism—the empowerment—of the Holy Spirit. John 1:12 declares that *"as many as received him, to them gave he power to become sons of God"* and you shall receive power after the Holy Spirit

The Prayer *That Works*

is come upon you, too. How shall you receive this gift? Repent and you will receive the gift of eternal life.

Precious reader, prepare your heart for the Holy Ghost baptism. It's nothing to be afraid of; you are just about to receive the ability to function maximally in this race. Please pray like this: *Father God, I believe that the promise of the Holy Spirit is for me. Now by faith I receive the Holy Spirit with the evidence of speaking with new—unknown—language/tongue*

Now, by faith, open your mouth and begin to speak! Speak loudly as long as possible. Expect to prophesy and magnify God.

Notes

Chapter One

1. Abi Olowe, *Great Revivals Great Revivalist: Joseph Ayo Babalola* (Houston: Omega Publishers, 2007), 289.

2. F. W. Boreham, "David Brainerd's Life Text," Wholesome Words, accessed November 1, 2011, http://www.wholesomewords.org/missions/biobrainerd6.html.

3. William Allen, *History of Revivals of Religion* (Antrim, N. Ireland: Revival Publishing,), 12. (Available in PDF format from The Revival Library at www.revival-library.org.)

Chapter Two

1. Edward Miller, *Cry for Me Argentina: Revival Begins in City Bell* (Essex, England: Sharon Publications, 1988), 11-17.

Chapter Three

1. Paraphrase of James 4:8.

2 Charles G. Finney, *The Autobiography of Charles G. Finney*, ed. Helen Wessel (Minneapolis: Bethany House, 1977), 125.

Notes

Chapter Five

1. L. G. Parkhurst, Jr., ed., *How To Pray in the Spirit: Thirty One Devotional Readings on Personal Prayer* (Grand Rapids: Kregel Publications, 1991), 6.

Chapter Six

1. "About Redemption Camp, The Redeemed Christian Church of God Redemption Camp," accessed November 1, 2011, http://city.rccgnet.org/about_redemption.html.

2. Roberts Liardon, ed., *John G. Lake: The Complete Collection of His Life Teachings* (New Kensington: Whitaker House, 1999), 227-228.

3. Wilford Reidt, *John G. Lake: A Man Without Compromise* (Tulsa: Harrison House, 1989), 27.

Chapter Seven

1. Roberts Liardon, *God's Generals: The Revivalists,* (New Kensington: Whitaker House, 2008), 308-309.

Acknowledgments

Special credit goes to those giants upon whose shoulders I have been able to stand in order to see afar. First of whom is Dr. D. K. Olukoya, the General Overseer of the Mountain of Fire and Miracles Ministries World Wide. He is a notable man of prayer. His ministry is crucial to the divine grace I operate in. I am not ashamed to identify myself with this great man of God and his ministry, under which I am privileged to serve as a minister.

Second, John Graham Lake (1870–1935) was said to be a man of prayer and commitment. I am constantly inspired and infused with great faith and a need to pray whenever I am privileged to read any of his writings. The boldness and assurance at which he conveyed the truth of the Scriptures is one of a kind. He could present the proofs of a praying man through the results of his prayers. I am extremely grateful to those individuals who have made such evidences—-such as their teachings—-available to our generation.

Third, a great man who though dead still speaks—Edward McKendree Bounds. I was introduced to his works on prayer during the preparation of this book and what I read is profound! Oswald J. Smith of blessed memory refers to him as "Immortal Bounds." E. M. Bounds was a man of prayer whose most notable insights for me are that *the message is forceful because the man is forceful,* and *prayer is that which make a man.* We can only by the special grace of God walk in Bound's footsteps. Though his footsteps are big, may God Himself carry us through in this very hour of pressing and urgent need for real prayer—prayer that works!

About the Author

Ayodeji D. Olusanmi is a Nigerian who currently resides in the United Kingdom. He met the Lord in an indelible manner in 2007. Upon this salvation experience, his life has never been the same and has since been doing great things for the Lord.

With a mandate and passion to write, his writings have been a blessing to multitudes around the world. He has led various ministry group in different capacities and has a passion for the youth, taking them out of the hands of the enemy by preaching the word of God with boldness. He enjoys winning the lost at all cost and serves as a minister of the gospel at the Mountain of Fire Miracle Ministries, United Kingdom. The Mountain of Fire and Miracle Ministries is a notable praying ministry with apostolic signs as described throughout the Acts of the Apostles.

His first book, *The Testimony of a Youth*, explains the dramatic transformation in his heart and life once Jesus became His Lord and Saviour. A fascinating and inspiring story for every youth in search of hope and freedom.

Ayodeji's books are available at
Amazon.com
Eden.co.uk
BookDepository.co.uk

www.ingramcontent.com/pod-product-compliance
Lightning Source LLC
Chambersburg PA
CBHW052056070526
44584CB00017B/2210